Whose Money Is It, Anyway?

Whose Money Is It, Anyway?

Dr. John F. MacArthur, Jr.

WORD PUBLISHING

NASHVILLE

A Thomas Nelson Company

WHOSE MONEY IS IT, ANYWAY?
Dr. John F. MacArthur, Jr.

Unless otherwise indicated, Scripture quotations used in this book are
from the *New American Standard Bible* (NASB), copyright © 1960,
1962, 1963, 1971, 1973, 1975, and 1977 by the Lockman Foundation,
and are used by permission.

Scripture references identified as KJV are from
the *King James Version* of the Bible.

Scripture references identified as NKJV are from
the *New King James Version,* copyright © 1979, 1980, 1982
by Thomas Nelson, Inc. Used by permission.

Scripture references identified NIV are from
the *New International Version,* copyright © 1978
by the New York International Bible Society.
Used by permission of Zondervan Bible Publishers.

Scripture references identified TLB are from *The Living Bible,*
copyright © 1971 by Tyndale House Publishers, Wheaton, Ill.
Used by permission.

MacArthur, John, 1939–
  Whose money is it anyway? : a biblical guide to using God's wealth / by
John F. MacArthur
    p. cm.
  Includes index.
  ISBN 0-8499-5554-8
  1. Christian giving. 2. Christian giving—Biblical teaching. I. Title.

BV772.M258 2000
248'.6—dc21   00-026813   CIP

Printed in the United States of America
00 01 02 03 04 05 QPV 6 5 4 3 2 1

Contents

Introduction

I HAVE THOUGHT about writing another book on giving for some time now. The first one I wrote, *Giving God's Way,* was published by Tyndale House in 1978. But I've avoided doing another book because I had convinced myself no one would buy it. Why? Because most people feel bad enough about what they don't give and what they spend. So why would they buy a book that's going to make them feel worse, or show them how to give away more of their money from which they are so reluctant to be separated?

I don't want to make you feel worse, I want to make you feel better. But the path to feeling better is understanding what the Bible says about giving and spending.

So that's why I feel compelled to write a book that answers the rhetorical question *Whose Money Is It, Anyway?*

Let me tell you what I mean by that title. The credibility of our Christianity is at stake in the handling of our funds. That's why we must treat money as a stewardship. If your employer gives you one hundred dollars to buy something for him, and then demands an accounting of how you spent the money, you are going to take good care of the money. But if you have one hundred dollars of your own money, then you'll spend it how you please. But whose money is it really? The answer is, God's. So, if you have to give an account to your employer, how much more of an account will you have to give to God for how you spend His money?

But you have an enemy to your stewardship of God's money. The world wants to use all your money so that you don't have any left to give. Advertisers compete with each other to entice you to use your available money to buy their products. And if you don't have enough money, banks and loan institutions are willing to provide you credit so you can buy those products, which puts you into debt, further limiting your resources for giving. Undoubtedly we live in an indulgent, materialistic culture, and that takes a toll on our giving.

Do you realize that people spend 50 percent of their waking time thinking about money—how to get it, how to spend it, how to save it, how to invest it, or how to borrow it? There's a place for saving. There's a place for wise planning. There's a place for meeting your needs. But first you need to understand how to give, where to give, and how much to give. You also need to know what should motivate you to give, and what will happen to you if you do give and what will happen to you if you don't. Those are the questions I'm going to answer in this book.

We'll begin by looking at what God has to say about money in general. In the first chapter we'll look at the nature of money and examine more in-depth the lure of materialism. In chapter two we'll survey Scripture to see the biblical guidelines and warnings about money. Chapter three will focus on the essentials of biblical stewardship, including the biblical means of acquiring money. Chapter four will conclude our general examination of money by describing what attitude you should have about money.

Introduction

Chapter five begins our look at the specifics of biblical giving by providing a model for it. In that chapter we'll answer these questions: When should we give? Is anyone exempt from giving? How should we give? How much should we give? Chapter six is basically a survey of the biblical characteristics of giving. Chapter seven answers an important question that has generated much confusion over the years: Does the Bible teach tithing or voluntary giving as the proper method for believers today? Chapter eight defines biblical stewardship, and in the last chapter we'll conclude by examining the true path to prosperity.

I have included an appendix on a topic that is becoming more and more relevant as our country witnesses a proliferation of state-run lotteries. I call it "The Seductive Fantasy of Gambling" because it examines the get-rich-quick formulas that essentially rob people of money. And it states in a direct way why gambling is wrong and is not at all biblical, as some maintain it is.

Jesus said, "It is more blessed to give than to receive" (Acts 20:35). It's more blessed in every way. And when you give as God has commanded, you will find it liberating, rewarding, joyous, profoundly enriching, and leading to the true path of prosperity. Enjoy the journey.

The world worries and scrambles and works—
often to the point of exhaustion—to make sure it
has enough wealth. But that is so unnecessary
because our heavenly Father knows our needs and
promises to provide for us every day.

The Morality of Money

HAVING A PROPER VIEW OF MONEY and possessions and managing them scripturally are serious challenges that face all Christians. By God's providence, people are in varying financial situations, but we all have to deal with the same questions: What do we do with our resources? How should we spend our money? How much should we save and invest? Those questions constantly test the genuineness and integrity of our spiritual walk. How a believer handles the stewardship of his finances and possessions communicates much about his or her spiritual condition.

To underscore how important the subject of money and possessions is to God, sixteen of Christ's thirty-eight parables speak about how people should handle earthly treasure. In fact, our Lord taught more about such stewardship (one out of every ten verses in the Gospels) than about heaven and hell combined. The entire Bible contains more than two thousand references to wealth and property, twice as many as the total references to faith and prayer. What we do with the *things* God has given us is very important to Him.

THE NATURE OF MONEY

Money in itself is neither righteous nor evil—it is morally neutral. However, money is an accurate measure of one's morality. When we refer to money we are referring to our medium of economic exchange, something so vital that it defines how we live from day to day. In a cash-based society it might have been difficult to track one's use of money, but today a look over your checkbook ledger or credit card statement will easily reveal where your money goes. And where you spend your money determines where your heart is and what your life's priorities are (Matt. 6:20–21). Someone who sees the pattern of your spending can fairly well discern the moral direction of your life.

Contrary to the fact that money is amoral, conventional wisdom for centuries has believed money necessarily corrupts. But that assessment goes against normal experience and good logic. There are certainly corrupt wealthy people who manifest their corruption through the misuse of their wealth, but there are also the righteous wealthy who demonstrate their righteousness by the godly way they invest their wealth. Similarly, among the ranks of the poor there have always been those who are corrupt and those who are righteous. So, money doesn't necessarily corrupt. But the use of it does reveal the inherent internal corruption of people. Money is not the essential problem; it is simply an indicator of the real problem, which is a sinful heart.

Even some Christians have accepted the erroneous view that money corrupts and is the underlying cause for all of life's problems. They claim it is wrong for believers to have any more money than is necessary for life's essentials. More radical advocates of that position might urge that all Christians band together and place all their money into a common pot from which they can share it equally—in essence, they endorse a Christian form of communism.

Those who propound such an extreme position on money management will invariably cite Acts 2:44–45 for scriptural support: "And all those who had believed were together and had all things in common; and they began selling their property and possessions and were sharing them with all, as anyone might have need." But what the early church did in Acts 2 does not support any form of Christian communism. Among the early believers, there were some who had money, possessions, and property, and others who did not. When those who owned little or nothing had needs, those with the resources sometimes sold a portion of what they owned and gave the money to their needy fellow believers. The Book of Acts does not say the early church ever pooled its resources and distributed them equally among the members.

Thus from its earliest days, the church saw money as neither good nor bad, but as a gift from God that could daily provide for one's own needs and regularly meet the needs of others.

ALL RICHES COME FROM GOD

The Old Testament prophets set forth the truth that all wealth comes from God: "'The silver is Mine and the gold is Mine,' declares the LORD of hosts" (Hag. 2:8; cf. Job 28; Ps. 104:24). Because God, as creator of the earth, owns everything anyway, He certainly doesn't forbid mankind from using money. God granted man the wisdom and privilege to turn the earth's rich resources into valuable commodities and his own talents into marketable services. A natural result was the use of various metals from the earth to make coins, and the use of trees to make paper for currency. He wants us to wisely take advantage of the earth's natural resources for those and other economic purposes.

In Deuteronomy 8:18, God moves a step further: "But you shall remember the LORD your God, for it is He who is giving you power to make wealth. . . ." He has not only created the raw materials for wealth, but has also given us the mental and physical ability to gain wealth and to use it.

The Lord in His providence has made each human being unique, with differing abilities to earn money. As a result, people have written great books and composed outstanding pieces of music, painted memorable pictures, and produced stage and film masterpieces, designed engineering marvels, developed new businesses, and discovered indispensable technical advances, all of which have generated personal income and benefited the world's social and economic structures. Such efforts are all within the framework of God's creative purpose and sovereign plan for mankind's use of the earth's great wealth (cf. 1 Cor. 4:7).

God wants you to understand that money by itself is morally neutral and that He, as the ultimate source of it and all material goods, has distributed all wealth as a stewardship. We all manage God's wealth. Money and possessions then become tests of morality and pose these personal questions: What are you going to do with the wealth you have? Will you pass this crucial, ongoing test of your moral and spiritual life? Sadly, as we are about to see, many professed believers—especially in recent decades—have not been able to pass the test and have dishonored God.

FAILING THE TEST: THE LURE OF MATERIALISM

Although it is not sinful to have money and possessions, it is definitely sinful to hoard, worship, and covet them as symbols of prestige, and overindulge by building your life around them. Such attitudes have always been commonplace in the world, but during the past several generations they have also captured the church and become a major issue there. Evangelicalism, instead of being separate from the world and offering a distinct, godly alternative to the world's view of wealth, has instead become self-indulgent and enamored with materialism. I believe it is a disappointing, fearful thing that many professing Christians no longer seem willing to be the offscouring of the world (1 Cor. 4:13, KJV).

Twenty years ago John White wrote an influential book titled *The Golden Cow*, which is still very helpful today. In it he charged the mainstream evangelical church with the sin of worshiping the golden cow of materialism. One major remedy, as stated vividly by White, is for Christ to use His whip of chastening and, as it were, cleanse the temple all over again. The author further presented this satirical and sobering analysis, which is perhaps even more applicable now:

> Not a calf, if you please, but a cow. I call her a *golden* cow because her udders are engorged with liquid gold, especially in the West where she grazes in meadows lush with greenbacks. Her priests placate her by slaughtering godly principles upon whose blood she looks with tranquil satisfaction. Anxious rows of worshipers bow down before their buckets. Although the gold squirts endlessly the worshipers are trembling lest the supply of sacrificial victims should one day fail to appease her. . . .
>
> Fundamentalism is my mother. I was nurtured in her warm bosom. She cared for me with love and taught me all she knew. I owe her (humanly speaking) my life, my spiritual food and many of my early joys. She introduced me to the Savior and taught me to feed on the bread of life. Our relationship

wasn't all honey and roses, but she was the only mother I had.
I clung to her then and find it hard not to lean on her now. If
she let me down at times I'm old enough to realize that no
mother is perfect. But to find out that she was a whore, that
she let herself be used by mammon, was another matter. And
as the wider evangelical movement gradually took her place in
my life it was painful to make the same discovery twice.[1]

I believe materialism is an even more serious issue facing
contemporary churches today. So many church members are
like the rich fool who wanted to build bigger and bigger barns
(Luke 12:16–18). However, he was not a role model for believers. We will never present a righteous alternative to unbelievers if
we adopt the materialistic thoughts and practices of the world.

We can begin to stem the tide of materialism simply by
having biblical motives and balanced practices regarding the
pastor's compensation. John White offers this persuasive
insight into what ought to be done:

> What would be wrong with giving him [the pastor] fifty per-
> cent more than whatever sum seems reasonable? Are you afraid
> it might make *him* too money conscious? If so, what business
> did you have in appointing him? If you are in a position to
> pick a pastor, you should also know that God expects you to
> discern whether he has a weakness about money. And if he has
> a weakness about money, you should never have given him the
> responsibility of a pastorate (1 Tim. 3:3)!
>
> Some churches like to give high salaries because the pas-
> tor's standard of living will affect the kind of people who will
> attend. (Posh pastor; fancy congregation.) God is concerned
> with motives not with amounts. Do you resent the thought
> of your pastor having too much money? Then double his
> salary! Why? To show him you love him. But aren't there bet-

ter ways of showing love? Of course there are, but why not show him love in these ways too? Do you ask me what happens if the salary is too much for him? I answer, that's the pastor's problem. He could give more money away, for instance. Pray that he may have wisdom in handling what he doesn't need.[2]

All believers, not just pastors, need to realize it's not a question of how much money you have; it's a question of where your heart is and what you do with what you have.

We all need to examine our attitudes toward luxuries and necessities. Proverbs 30:8–9 says, "Give me neither poverty nor riches, but give me only my daily bread. Otherwise, I may have too much and disown you and say, 'Who is the Lord?' Or I may become poor and steal, and so dishonor the name of my God" (NIV). Wealth or the lack of it is a constant test for us. If we have more than we need, we'll be tempted not to trust God. If we don't have enough, we'll be tempted to dishonor His name. The key to passing the test of wealth is simply found in trusting God, who is infinitely greater than all the wealth in the universe.

PASSING THE TEST:
THE TREASURE OF CONTENTMENT

The dictionary defines contented as "feeling or manifesting satisfaction with one's possessions, status, or situation." For the Christian, however, a definition of contentment goes far beyond the issues of worldly wealth and success. You'll find real contentment in God as you realize that your heavenly Father owns everything, controls everything, and provides everything. Wholeheartedly embracing these truths will begin to lead to victory over the pervasive snare of materialism.

God Owns Everything

God is the sole proprietor of everything you have—your clothes, your house, your car, your children, your computer, your CD player, your investments, your sports equipment, your lawn and garden—and everything else imaginable. King David affirmed that truth several times: "For all that is in heaven and in earth is Yours. . . . Both riches and honor come from You, and You reign over all" (1 Chron. 29:11, 12, NKJV); "The earth is the LORD's, and all it contains, the world, and those who dwell in it" (Ps. 24:1).

Since God owns everything, you can never really acquire anything new because it is already His. Embracing this fact is crucial in attaining a biblical attitude of contentment.

Either from your own perspective or God's, you have to deal with your possessions. As long as they belong to Him, you should stop worrying and let Him take care of them. That's the way John Wesley reacted one day when he received the news that fire had destroyed his house. He simply said, "The Lord's house burned down. One less responsibility for me."

Wesley's approach was the right one, but it is not how the world teaches us to respond. The self-centered accumulation of property is the world's legacy to us, but we need to change that perspective. *We do not own anything.* Therefore, if you ever lose something, you don't really lose it, because you never owned it. If someone needs some of what you have, he may be as entitled to it as you are, because you don't own it—God does.

God Controls Everything

It follows that if God owns everything, He also controls everything. The Old Testament emphasizes the fact that God sovereignly controls all circumstances for His own ends.

Isaiah 46:9–10 says, "Remember the former things long past, for I am God, and there is no other; I am God, and there is no one like Me, declaring the end from the beginning, and from ancient times things which have not been done, saying, 'My purpose will be established, and I will accomplish all My good pleasure'" (cf. 1 Chron. 29:11–12; Job 23:13; Ps. 33:11; Prov. 16:9; 21:1, 30).

Daniel expressed the same idea when he thanked and blessed God for revealing to him the meaning of the king's dream: "Let the name of God be blessed forever and ever, for wisdom and power belong to Him. It is He who changes the times and the epochs; He removes kings and establishes kings; He gives wisdom to wise men and knowledge to men of understanding. It is He who reveals the profound and hidden things; He knows what is in the darkness, and the light dwells with Him" (Dan. 2:20–22).

That same kind of theology sustained Daniel when he was cast into the lions' den (Dan. 6). In spite of the perilous circumstances of being surrounded by hungry lions, Daniel apparently had a relatively easy time in the pit. Verse 23 reports, "Daniel was taken up out of the den and no injury whatever was found on him, because he had trusted in his God."

Meanwhile, King Darius had spent the night in perfect circumstances in his royal palace, yet he couldn't eat, sleep, drink, or be entertained. Why such an improbable contrast between Daniel and the king? Because Daniel had a confident faith that God was in sovereign control of everything. Darius was nervous and shaken because he did not know the divine Controller and believed circumstances were spinning out of his own control.

If Daniel could trust in God's control over a life-threatening situation, you can trust in His control over all your circumstances—even down to the smallest financial concern.

God Provides Everything

God owns all resources and controls every circumstance so that He is able to provide for every need of His people. The apostle Paul assured the Philippian church that "my God will supply all your needs according to His riches in glory in Christ Jesus" (Phil. 4:19, NASB).

One of the most lovely Hebrew names for God is *Jehovah-jireh,* "the LORD who provides" (Gen. 22:14). God's provision for those who trust in Him is so characteristic of His nature that it is one of His names. You may never doubt most of God's attributes (for example, His holiness, love, goodness, power, justice, and glory), but you may at times wonder whether or not He will provide your needs. However, that is exactly what Jesus cautioned His followers against in Matthew 6:25–34 when He said they should not worry about what to eat, drink, or wear.

God is still *Jehovah-jireh,* the God who provides, and that is why David said, "I have not seen the righteous forsaken or his descendants begging bread" (Ps. 37:25). A paraphrase of Luke 12:30 says, "All mankind scratches for its daily bread" (TLB). The world worries and scrambles and works—often to the point of exhaustion—to make sure it has enough wealth. But that is so unnecessary because our heavenly Father knows our needs and promises to provide for us every day.

If you know God owns everything in the world, controls all its assets, and can provide for you as His child, then there is no need for you to trust in luxury, be enticed by materialism, or stockpile for the future. Your daily life as a Christian need not revolve around those concerns, but in being content with what you have (1 Tim. 6:6–8; Heb. 13:5). You don't have to own everything or be in control of every circumstance to have enough money for your basic needs. Instead, you can set aside all worry and anxiety about your needs and gladly receive whatever God gives you to invest in His kingdom (Matt. 6:31–34). That's the scriptural answer to how we should view wealth and how we should start to deal with any prideful, selfish preoccupation with greed and materialism.

2

"Beware that you do not forget the LORD your God by not keeping His commandments and His ordinances and His statutes which I am commanding you today; otherwise, when you have eaten and are satisfied, and have built good houses and lived in them, and when your herds and your flocks multiply, and your silver and gold multiply, and all that you have multiplies, then your heart will become proud and you will forget the LORD your God. . . ."

—Deuteronomy 8:11–14

Guidelines and Warnings about Money

"SHOW ME THE MONEY!" That short, crass exclamation from a popular 1990s film fairly well captures the spirit of the age in contemporary Western societies. Through continual reminders of it in everyday conversations and mass media advertising, money has become a powerful and constant element in our lives. Such an all-consuming concern for money is what drives most people in the world.

It's wrong and counterproductive to have that as your primary vocational motivation. Everyone, believers and unbelievers alike, should rather strive to excel in his or her vocation and let the rewards come. Here are the kinds of thoughts that should drive your actions: *No matter what job or profession I have, I'm not going to settle for anything less than the maximum expression of my ability. My primary concern is not going to be what my pay is, but what my effort is—how carefully, efficiently, and excellently I work.* (cf. Eph. 6:5–7; Col. 3:22–24.)

But so many people, contrary to the clear teaching of God's Word, just pursue the money from their jobs and not the excellence of *doing* their jobs. They ignore or are unaware of the apostle Paul's admonition: "Instruct those who are rich in this present world not to be conceited or to fix their hope on the uncertainty of riches, but on God, who richly supplies us with all things to enjoy" (1 Tim. 6:17). They are proud of their possessions and their status, and they are deriving their security from materialism, which is a form of idolatry.

Even Christians are sometimes guilty of such idolatry, whereas they should agree with the psalmist and say, "As the deer pants for the water brooks, so my soul pants for You, O God" (Ps. 42:1). The sin of deriving all personal joy from wealth rather than from God is so unnecessary if you just remember Jesus' warning, "No servant can serve two masters; for either he will hate the one and love the other, or else he will be devoted to one and despise the other. You cannot serve God and wealth" (Luke 16:13; cf. Matt. 6:24). To serve God, you must obey His command, "But seek first His kingdom and His righteousness, and all these things will be added to you" (Matt. 6:33). Inherent in both of the preceding admonitions is the truth that Jesus related one's attitude toward money by the genuineness of his or her relationship to God. If you fully understand that, you will more than likely avoid the idolatry of materialism.

JESUS' GUIDELINES ON MONEY AND SALVATION

Christ's teaching on money encompasses some of the most well-known and striking stories in the Gospels. Before we look at them, it should be noted that they are not isolated accounts or inconsistent with what the rest of the New Testament teaches about money and spirituality. For instance, when the crowds asked John the Baptist, the forerunner of the Messiah, what the fruit of repentance included, he said this:

"The man who has two tunics is to share with him who has none; and he who has food is to do likewise." And some tax collectors also came to be baptized, and they said to him, "Teacher, what shall we do?" And he said to them, "Collect no more than what you have been ordered to." Some soldiers were questioning him, saying, "And what about us, what shall we do?" And he said to them, "Do not take money from anyone by force, or accuse anyone falsely, and be content with your wages." (Luke 3:11–14)

After the birth of the church, members manifested their spiritual transformation by a willingness to sell their property and give the proceeds to others in the church who had need (Acts 2:44–45; 4:32–37). Furthermore, the Book of Acts records how the Ephesian occultists confirmed the reality of their conversions by willingly burning their valuable books on magic (19:17–20).

The following selections from Jesus' teachings on money and possessions demonstrate that He was in complete agreement with God's will on this vital topic. The first two stories show how positive and negative attitudes on wealth are related to salvation. The second set of contrasting examples will reveal what Jesus considered to be lifestyles of foolish and wise stewardship.

Money: An Indicator of Salvation

Jesus repeatedly linked money to a person's most fundamental spiritual condition—his salvation. For example, the story of Zaccheus' conversion in Luke 19:1–10 provides insight into how a wealthy tax collector's spiritual turnaround also resulted in a transformed attitude about money.

Zaccheus' inquisitive glimpse of Jesus from a tree began

an amazing sequence of events. The Lord greeted him, confronted his sin, and told him of spiritual need. Zaccheus then repented of that sin and embraced his Savior. Immediately the rich tax gatherer pledged half his money to the poor and promised to reimburse fourfold anyone he had defrauded.

Zaccheus' salvation immediately affected the financial area of his life. The initial evidence of his transformed life was his completely changed attitude toward his money. As a tax collector in the Roman Empire, he had been totally focused on accumulating as much wealth as possible, even if it meant defrauding taxpayers and withholding contributions to people in need.

Zaccheus' transformation was so genuine and dramatic that Jesus made this clear-cut declaration, "Today salvation has come to this house" (Luke 19:9, NASB). Our Lord was judging the reality of that man's salvation by his cheerful eagerness to part with his money for the glory of God and the good of others.

However, not all such encounters with Jesus had a positive outcome. The Synoptic Gospels (Matt. 19; Mark 10; Luke 18) each contain the story of the rich young ruler. He was a devout Jew, a ruler in the synagogue who professed careful obedience to the Ten Commandments since his youth—by today's description, a typical hard working, decent, sincere urban professional.

Quite amazingly, when he came to Jesus to find out how to obtain eternal life, Christ did not give him a profound theological discourse on what it means to be saved. Instead, He urged him to obey God completely and demonstrate one important fruit of true repentance: obedience to Christ's commands. And the Lord picked a command that would reveal whether he really was repentant concerning salvation. Jesus said to him, "One thing you lack: go and sell all you possess and give to the poor, and you will have treasure in heaven; and come, follow Me" (Mark 10:21).

Sadly, the young man—unwilling to obey Christ if it meant parting with his wealth—left, averse to following Jesus' instructions. He had to turn away from eternal life because he could not bring himself to relinquish any of his riches, even if the Lord and Savior commanded it.

Jesus then gave the disciples a brief and perhaps rather startling commentary on the incident. He told them it is easier for a camel to go through the eye of a needle—which, of course, is impossible—than for a rich man to enter heaven while trusting in his riches. Love of wealth presents an impassable barrier to regeneration because the desire for riches is greater than the desire for forgiveness and heaven, as in the case of the young ruler.

Those two significant occasions in which Jesus closely related one's attitude toward money with one's status before God stand in sharp contrast to each other. In the story of Zaccheus, the fact that his attitude toward wealth changed was solid evidence that his repentance and seeking after God were genuine. In the story of the rich young ruler, his stubborn refusal to let go of his wealth was evidence of his worship of self.

Money: An Index to Spiritual Health

People can waste their money and their lives by directing all their wealth into temporal, earthly investments. History records in the words of famous wealthy people, that there is no joy in such a life. John D. Rockefeller lamented, "I have made many millions, but they have brought me no happiness." Cornelius Vanderbilt commented, "The care of millions is too great a load . . . there is no pleasure in it." John

Jacob Astor once called himself "the most miserable man on earth." And Henry Ford looked back to a more care free time when he "was happier doing mechanic's work."

In the parable of the rich fool (Luke 12:15–21), Jesus focused on the wealthy person's dissatisfaction with what he has. In this case, the rich man demonstrated a completely unbalanced, greedy approach toward the stewardship of his possessions.

Luke's text does not say how the man became rich, and we don't have to assume that he succeeded in business dishonestly. We can reasonably infer that he was simply a businessman who worked diligently to build his business and reached a point at which he wanted to expand it. So far, there is nothing wrong with that—not even with his goal to be at ease in the future and "eat, drink, and be merry" (v. 19). God is not opposed to our normal enjoyment of all the rich aspects of His marvelous creation.

But the problem with the rich man's way of doing business was his obsessive focus on personal economic security and comfortable retirement. God viewed his approach with such disfavor that he called him a fool. The folly was that the man had been so totally consumed in preparing for his temporal comfort that he had given no thought to preparing for his eternal well being. The consequences of such foolishness are very harsh and sobering: "'This very night your soul is required of you; and now who will own what you have prepared?' So is the man who stores up treasure for himself, and is not rich toward God" (Luke 12:20–21).

By contrast, Jesus showed his disciples an example of wise stewardship by one who had her priorities in godly order:

And He sat down opposite the treasury, and began observing how the people were putting money into the treasury; and

22

many rich people were putting in large sums. And a poor widow came and put in two small copper coins, which amount to a cent. Calling His disciples to Him, He said to them, "Truly I say to you, this poor widow put in more than all the contributors to the treasury; for they all put in out of their surplus, but she, out of her poverty, put in all she owned, all she had to live on" (Mark 12:14–44).

As extreme as the widow's action was, Jesus did not question its wisdom or motivation. Instead, He gave her an unqualified commendation, telling the twelve apostles and us that she was wise and a model of good stewardship. In fact, He enshrined her as the all-time example of godly generosity, commitment, and sacrificial giving.

So our Lord called the rich man foolish and the poor widow wise. It is better to have everything in heaven and nothing here than everything here and nothing for eternity. Jesus was again leading to the conclusion that how you handle money is a litmus test or index of your spiritual condition.

Concerning the wealthy donors in Mark 12, Jesus assessed their spiritual health in a very deliberate way. The text says, "He sat down opposite the treasury, and began observing how the people were putting money into the treasury" (v. 41). It does not say He was just passing by and happened to glance and notice somebody giving something. He was in the area of the temple treasury with the purpose of intentionally watching what people gave. And He is still watching with serious concern what you and I give because the nature of our giving reveals so much about our spiritual character.

Thus Jesus both wounds and heals with His various teachings about money. His words on the subject are best

23

summarized by what He said in the Sermon on the Mount, "Do not store up for yourselves treasures on earth, where moth and rust destroy, and where thieves break in and steal. But store up for yourselves treasures in heaven, where moth and rust do not destroy, and where thieves do not break in and steal; for where your treasure is, there your heart will be also" (Matt. 6:19–21, NIV). Implicit in that final statement is a warning against letting your wealth guide your affections—a warning issued even more explicitly by the apostle Paul.

THE WARNING AGAINST LOVING MONEY

Paul provides the New Testament's clearest, most direct warning against loving wealth: "For the love of money is a root of all sorts of evil, and some by longing for it have wandered away from the faith and pierced themselves with many griefs" (1 Tim. 6:10). He wrote that as one instruction in a series to leaders in the church, and specifically to warn against one characteristic of false teachers. True leaders and teachers must avoid the greed of false teachers, as must all believers. So Paul was constrained to warn us about the sin of greed and materialism.

Red Flags Regarding the Love of Money

When a person is a lover of money, one or more of the following danger signs will often appear. First, the person will be bent on making money any way possible. He may have little regard for using only honest means or working hard. Christians, on the other hand, will strive to work honestly and with diligent excellence, knowing that God may reward them with abundant earnings, but that He is not so obligated.

Second, a person is a lover of money if he never seems to

24

have enough. He is like the leech's daughters who constantly say "Give, Give" (Prov. 30:15). But the one freed from such enslavement will agree with Paul, "I have learned to be content in whatever circumstances I am" (Phil. 4:11).

Third, if someone loves money, he will likely flaunt it. He derives inordinate pleasure in showing off his luxury purchases—and today many of those likely were made with an overextended credit card.

Fourth, lovers of money usually hate to give it to others, no matter how much those people might need it. Money lovers would rather spend all they have on themselves to meet their own desires. And if they give any money at all it is usually a small amount given with the intent of bringing them some honor.

The final red flag, closely related to the first one, is that people who love money are often willing to sin to acquire more or keep as much as they can of what they have. They may lie on their tax returns, pad their expense accounts, or steal from their workplace. They are willing to compromise their principles for riches, which reveals a heart that loves money more than God, righteousness, and truth.

The Effects of Loving Money

If the preceding warning signals reliably identify those plagued by the sin of money love, the following negative effects are even more certain to result from greed and materialism. First, the one who loves money will trust in it rather than God. He looks with satisfaction to his bulging bank accounts. He takes great comfort in his diversified investment portfolio. He is glad for his abundant salary and perhaps boasts about certain bonuses or incentives he receives. He rests in the security of having more than enough insurance to meet every possible contingency. Finally, the one who trusts supremely in his money sits back and thinks to himself, *I've got all the money I need for a rainy day. I'm covered on every front. I can take care of myself.*

If that describes you, you need to ask if you are trusting in God or in your gold. It is not wrong to be prudent about savings, investments, and insurance, but it is wrong to trust in them more than in God. Job knew the dangers involved:

> If I have put my confidence in gold, and called fine gold my trust, if I have gloated because my wealth was great, and because my hand had secured so much; if I have looked at the sun when it shone or the moon going in splendor, and my heart became secretly enticed, and my hand threw a kiss from my mouth, that too would have been an iniquity calling for judgment, for I would have denied God above. (Job 31:24–28; cf. Prov. 11:28; 1 Tim. 6:17–18)

Second, another certain result of loving money is deception, or a false sense of security. Jesus refers to this in the parable of the soils (Matt. 13:22; Mark 4:19; cf. Luke 8:14). Riches can choke the Word and deceive you about spiritual reality. If you feel secure in the knowledge that you have plenty of money, you may begin to think you have all you need and that all is well.

False teachers appeal directly to the deception of riches and to those who trust in money for their security. Advocates of the prosperity gospel claim that if you're rich that means you're extra special to God and He will shower you with abundant favors. And the way to become rich is to send money to the prosperity preacher. The more you send, the richer you will be. Furthermore, according to them, the more wealth you have, the more God has favored you. It's not uncommon for someone in that movement to refute charges against such false teachers by asking, "How can you say our leader is a false teacher? God has made him so wealthy, so He must be pleased with him and his teaching, right?" Such is the vicious circle that makes the false teacher rich and impoverishes the followers.

A third inevitable effect of loving money is that it leads you to build your life on a fleeting, unstable foundation. Proverbs 23:4–5 says, "Do not weary yourself to gain wealth, cease from your consideration of it. When you set your eyes on it, it is gone. For wealth certainly makes itself wings like an eagle that flies toward the heavens." Money is a very uncertain and unpredictable commodity in your life. Just when you think you can count on it, it's gone. Building your life on money is as foolish and unsteady as building a house on the sand— changing conditions undermine the foundation and can cause it to shift or sink at any time. The only stable foundation for your life is the truth, which teaches you to love God and seek to glorify His name (cf. Matt. 7:24–27).

Fourth, the love of money is also certain to make you proud. The writer of Proverbs states the case accurately and succinctly, "The rich man is wise in his own conceit" (28:11, KJV). If you're enthralled with wealth and successful at amassing it, it's easy to feel self-sufficient, smug, and superior to those who have less than you do. However, Deuteronomy 8:11–14 warns God's people against being proud in their wealth:

> Beware that you do not forget the LORD your God by not keeping His commandments and His ordinances and His statutes which I am commanding you today; otherwise, when you have eaten and are satisfied, and have built good houses and lived in them, and when your herds and your flocks multiply, and your silver and gold multiply, and all

that you have multiplies, then your heart will become proud and you will forget the LORD your God. . . ."

Unless you maintain a biblical perspective on riches and deal with pride, you will succumb to arrogance concerning your wealth, as Ephraim did: "And Ephraim said, 'Surely I have become rich, I have found wealth for myself; in all my labors they will find in me no iniquity, which would be sin'" (Hos. 12:8).

Fifth, the love of money, which is idolatry, will invariably cause you to steal from God. That means in your stewardship of money and possessions you will not do what is right; you will not render to God what is His. The people of Malachi's time were guilty of stealing from God: "Will a man rob God? Yet you are robbing Me! But you say, 'How have we robbed You?' In tithes and offerings" (Mal. 3:8).

As absurd as the question of robbing God sounded, the prophet had to ask it. And he answered his own question with a resounding yes. When the people, who obviously loved their money too much, asked how they were stealing from God, Malachi simply answered, "In tithes and offerings." In other words, they hadn't given God all that was rightfully His.

There was a very clear remedy for that sinful situation. "'Bring the whole tithe into the storehouse, so that there may be food in My house, and test Me now in this,' says the LORD of hosts, 'if I will not open for you the windows of heaven and pour out for you a blessing until it overflows'" (Mal. 3:10).

If you are a slave to the love of money, you need to have the same kind of response Malachi commanded for his listeners. You may think you are not stealing from God and that you never will, but if you are not placing a generous portion of your resources into God's kingdom, you are robbing Him.

Finally, if you love money you will not only steal from God, you will steal from others. First John 3:17 makes this crystal clear, "But whoever has the world's goods, and sees his brother in need and closes his heart against him, how does the love of God abide in him?" Romans 5:5 says, "the love of God has been poured out within our hearts through the Holy Spirit who was given to us." Here Paul proclaims one of the major identifying marks of the believer (cf. 1 John 3:14). Paul and John move our discussion beyond the mere consideration of excessive love for riches. The more important question becomes, "If you refuse to give money to someone in need (especially to a brother or sister in Christ), how can you claim to be a Christian?"

Loving money will make you behave like an unbeliever. Or, as the apostle John raised the possibility, it may reveal that you are not a believer at all. That's what it all comes down to, which is why you need to examine your life regularly (2 Cor. 13:5) and strive to be free from the love of money.

You are to pursue God, not wealth. Like David, you should be able to say, "As for me, I shall behold Your face in righteousness; I will be satisfied with Your likeness when I awake" (Ps. 17:15).

One exemplary believer who reached that level of satisfaction early in his Christian life was C. T. Studd. He was one of nineteenth-century England's greatest cricket stars who became a Christian and left his athletic career for missionary service. Prior to departing for the mission field, Studd resolved to give away his rather substantial inheritance. His biographer provides the details:

> So far as he could judge, his inheritance was £29,000. But in order to leave a margin for error, he decided to start by giving £25,000. One memorable day, Jan. 13, 1887, he sent off four

cheques of £5,000 each, and five of £1,000. . . . This was no fool's plunge on his part. It was his public testimony before God and man that he believed God's Word to be the surest thing on earth, and that the hundredfold interest which God has promised in this life, not to speak of the next, is an actual reality for those who believe it and act on it.

He sent £5,000 to Mr. [D. L.] Moody, expressing the hope that he would be able to start some Gospel Work at Tirhoot in North India, where his father had made his fortune. Moody hoped to carry this out, but was unable to, and instead used the money to start the famous Moody Bible Institute in Chicago. . . .

£5,000 he sent to Mr. George Müller, £4,000 to be used on missionary work, and £1,000 among the orphans; £5,000 to George Holland, in Whitechapel, "to be used for the Lord among His poor in London," . . . and £5,000 to Commissioner Booth Tucker for the Salvation Army in India.[1]

Studd gave the remainder of the £25,000 to various other organizations. The original inheritance total of £29,000 was actually a few thousand pounds short of the real total, so he gave some of that money to additional organizations and the rest as a gift to his fianceé. She, in turn, gave away that portion of the money. When the couple went to Africa as missionaries, they had no money.

"It is the blessing of the LORD that makes rich, and He adds no sorrow to it."

—Proverbs 10:22

3 The Essentials of Biblical Stewardship

TODAY'S CHRISTIAN AUTHORS have produced a number of books and articles advocating semi-poverty for believers. The argument goes that if you are a truly dedicated Christian you will shun the love of money, avoid all material comfort, and be satisfied with nothing more than the bare economic necessities. For historical precedent, this viewpoint sometimes cites examples of medieval monastic orders (for example, the Franciscans) that encouraged members to live austere lives, separated from the excesses of worldly wealth. Advocates of "Christian poverty" will even reason along these lines concerning Jesus' ministry lifestyle: "Jesus was poor and homeless, and if our Lord was called to poverty, shouldn't we, His followers, emulate His lifestyle? After all, it must be God's best for the believer, and He'll provide all the basics of life that we need."

But is that argument valid? Is it even based on biblical fact, and does it accurately reflect God's purpose for us? I believe the answer to all those questions is no, and Scripture demonstrates why in ways that might surprise those who think Christian poverty leads to righteousness.

JESUS' TRUE ECONOMIC SITUATION

The assertion that Jesus grew up with the poor and was homeless is simply not true. A brief overview of Israel's socio-economic structure at the time of His incarnation may help us better understand His actual status. At the lowest level was a rather large segment of poor people, about which Jesus told the disciples, "For you always have the poor with you" (Matt. 26:11, NASB). He did not despise them; He knew they would always be present and in need of believers' love and generosity (cf. Deut. 15:11).

Then, as in most countries, Israel had a small but influential upper class of wealthy people. They were the landowners and religious leaders, those who wielded power and authority under the direction of the occupying Romans.

At the time of Christ, in the center of Jewish society was a significant middle class composed of craftsmen and tradesmen. This segment included farmers, toolmakers, pottery makers, builders, and other artisans. Jesus was born into such a middle-class family. His earthly father Joseph had his own construction business. We usually translate the Greek word for his occupation "carpenter," but it is more precisely rendered "builder." The meaning includes one who is a brick mason, or one who works with wood.

Joseph had quite a number of children in addition to Jesus and certainly must have made enough money to support them. According to historians, construction was flourishing in and around Nazareth of Galilee, Jesus' hometown. That was due to Roman expansion and the area's location near the major east-west, north-south trade routes of that day. So it's likely that Joseph was a good carpenter who took advantage of the many construction opportunities around Nazareth and, with Jesus' help, built a thriving business. And Jesus, as the firstborn son, would have inherited the family business after Joseph died.

It's therefore wrong to conclude that Jesus entered the world as a poor and homeless individual who led a poverty-stricken life. He grew up in a middle-class family that enjoyed some of the comforts that living in Galilee provided—a great supply of natural resources, abundant food and water, and beautiful scenery. It was only after He began His itinerant ministry that Christ depended on the love and care of others for food, a place to stay, and so forth. That is not much different from how most modern missionaries and traveling evangelists operate.

Instead of assuming that Jesus was poor and somehow encouraged His followers to live likewise, I believe we ought to recognize His middle-class birth and upbringing and seriously consider God's purpose behind it. The Father very likely sent the Son to a middle-class working environment where He could thoughtfully and wisely speak to the wealthy and also comfort and understand the poor. Jesus would have been able to identify fairly well with each of the other classes.

ALL THINGS RICHLY TO ENJOY

In further refuting any notion that poverty or asceticism is God's ideal standard for you and me, it's refreshing and reassuring to reflect again on these words of this well-known hymn:

This is my Father's world, and to my listening ears
All nature sings, and round me rings the music of the
spheres.
This is my Father's world: I rest me in the thought
Of rocks and trees, of skies and seas—His hand the wonders
wrought.

35

The description of the Garden of Eden shows some of the lavish riches God provided for man's enjoyment:

> The LORD God planted a garden toward the east, in Eden; and there He placed the man whom He had formed. Out of the ground the LORD God caused to grow every tree that is pleasing to the sight and good for food; the tree of life also in the midst of the garden, and the tree of the knowledge of good and evil. Now a river flowed out of Eden to water the garden; and from there it divided and became four rivers. The name of the first is Pishon; it flows around the whole land of Havilah, where there is gold. The gold of that land is good; the bdellium and the onyx stone are there. The name of the second river is Gihon; it flows around the whole land of Cush. The name of the third river is Tigris; it flows east of Assyria. And the fourth river is the Euphrates. (Gen. 2:8–14)

God had indeed created a natural world—one that was rich and beautiful but nevertheless became through the Fall cursed and perishing. The earth is a relatively young planet (a proper understanding of science and Scripture would make it about six thousand years old), designed by God in the midst of eternity for a very brief purpose. According to the divine timetable, in the near future the present world will become extinct (cf. Matt. 5:18; 2 Pet. 3:10–13), and be replaced by a new heaven and a new earth (Rev. 21:1). The present earth, as it reveals the nature of its Creator, is simply for mankind's temporary use and enjoyment. The earth itself possesses no sacred or eternal characteristics; therefore we can enjoy and wisely utilize all its beautiful physical traits and rich natural resources.

When God created the universe, He made a very important distinction between man and the rest of creation. Except for man, all of creation—animate and inanimate—is temporary, without a soul, and passing into oblivion. But men and women are eternal beings, made in the very image of God—superior in design, value, capability, responsibility, and authority over the rest of creation. Genesis 1:27–29 says,

> God created man in His own image, in the image of God He created him; male and female He created them. God blessed them; and God said to them, "Be fruitful and multiply, and fill the earth, and subdue it; and rule over the fish of the sea and the birds of the sky and over every living thing that moves on the earth." Then God said, "Behold, I have given you every plant yielding seed that is on the surface of all the earth, and every tree which has fruit yielding seed; it shall be food for you.

This passage contains a very important command from God. He has given man sovereignty over all the other elements of creation. We are to harness all of earth's power, beauty, productivity, and rich capabilities. As one writer notes, "It is here to be exploited, studied, cultivated, tamed, used, and enjoyed." The whole earth and all it contains is to provide for us in this life.

When you think about it, the beauty of nature is quite staggering—its breathtaking splendor is part of God's good gift to man. A wonderful example of this is when the leaves turn colors each autumn in certain regions of the world. One such area famous for its brilliant fall colors is the northeastern United States, especially the New England states. Author Bill Bryson describes just how beautiful an autumn day in New England can be:

> Yesterday, under the pretense of doing vital research, I drove over to Vermont and treated my startled feet to a hike up

Killington Peak, 4,235 feet of sturdy splendor in the heart of the Green Mountains. It was one of those sumptuous days when the world is full of autumn muskiness and tangy, crisp perfection: vivid blue sky, deep green fields, leaves in a thousand luminous hues. It is a truly astounding sight when every tree in the landscape becomes individual, when each winding back highway and plump hillside is suddenly and infinitely splashed with every sharp shade that nature can bestow—flaming scarlet, lustrous gold, throbbing vermilion, fiery orange.

Forgive me if I seem a tad effusive, but it is impossible to describe a spectacle this grand without babbling. Even the great naturalist Donald Culross Peattie, whose prose is so dry you could use it to mop spills, totally lost his head when he tried to convey the wonder of a New England autumn.

The language of Peattie's classic *Natural History of Trees of Eastern and Central North America* can most generously be called workmanlike; but when he turns his attention to the sugar maple and its vivid autumnal regalia, out tumble breathless metaphors. For example, he likens the maple's colors to "the shout of a great army . . . these falling tongues of maple fire . . . like the mighty, marching melody that rides upon the crest of some symphonic weltering sea and, with its crying song, gives meaning to all the calculated dissonance of the orchestra.". . . .

When I reached the preternaturally clear air of Killington's summit, with views to every horizon soaked in autumn luster, I found it was all I could do not to fling open my arms and burst forth with a medley of . . . tunes.[1]

If you're a believer, you know that the kind of magnificent scenery Bill Bryson witnessed demonstrates God's loving, generous, almost lavish character. You should have an even greater sense of awe over it than Bryson did as you thank, praise, and glorify God the Creator. Such enriching experiences ought to cause you to obey Him who is so generous, because it should stimulate in you a foretaste of heaven. Whatever the wonders, joys, comforts, and beauties of this world are, they are but a small preview of those we will enjoy in the world to come.

Thus God through Scripture and general revelation provides an unmistakable affirmation of the goodness of this disposable planet. When you combine the richness of the earth with mankind's God-given ability to cultivate (raising livestock and grains), enjoy limitless tastes and smells, and extract (retrieving valuable metals, gems, minerals, and fuels) that richness, you have the fulfillment of God's purpose for men and women to enjoy life. The earth's wealth and beauty are here for just a short time, but God says you and I are to enjoy it all while it lasts.

As with everything else, however, the earth's goodness and our enjoyment and use of it have been seriously marred by sin. Adam and Eve sinned and the curse fell on the earth. God originally gave them the freedom to manage everything in the Garden of Eden. God still allows mankind freedom to use the earth's resources, but sadly people abuse those good things and turn them into products of destruction (weapons that maim and kill, narcotics and poisons that destroy people's lives). Or they turn these resources into material gods and in effect worship those instead of the true God.

But even with mankind's sinful excesses in handling the world's goods, God does not command us to stop using and enjoying them. The sin is not in enjoying the earth's bounty. The sin is overindulgence and waste—flaunting your wealth and engaging in a self-centered, compassionless consumption.

The scriptural, godly approach is to have the right heart attitude in partaking of God's many material blessings. If you enjoy them, give Him thanks, and become willing to share generously with others. Then you have made righteous use of the wealth God has entrusted to you.

GOD-HONORING WAYS OF ACQUIRING MONEY

Do we have a right to acquire and enjoy wealth? I trust we have made it clear that the answer is yes. If you're diligent and you have a grateful, obedient attitude that trusts God and His Word, it may be His will to reward you financially to some degree. The Lord has your best interests in mind. Proverbs 10:22 says, "It is the blessing of the LORD that makes rich, and He adds no sorrow to it." (I'm not saying it's God's will for all believers to be equally wealthy and never encounter difficulties. I'm simply reiterating that it is not inherently wrong for you or me to take advantage of the material opportunities He has set before us.)

Acquiring Money through Work

That conclusion leads inevitably to another question: If God declares it okay to enjoy some measure of wealth, how do we obtain it? The answer is straightforward and uncomplicated. First of all, the most familiar way to acquire money— although probably not the most popular—is to work for it.

Work is not only the primary way to acquire money, it is God's gift to mankind and actually commanded by Him. "Six days you shall labor and do all your work, but the seventh day is a sabbath of the LORD your God; in it you shall not do any work . . ." (Exod. 20:9–10). God has provided six days for us to work, and He has reserved one day for us to rest and worship Him.

"He who steals must steal no longer; but rather he must

labor, performing with his own hands what is good . . ." (Eph. 4:28). Hard work brings self-respect, allows you to use your human talents and abilities productively, and has God's approval as opposed to unrighteous means (theft, etc.) of obtaining wealth. Work also keeps you from being idle, wasting your time, and falling into all kinds of temptation.

Proverbs 28:19 extols the virtue of work, "He who tills his land will have plenty of food, but he who follows empty pursuits will have poverty in plenty." If you want to be poor, chase the wind or follow after unproven schemes and irrational dreams. On the other hand, one proven way to have plenty is to work for it.

The Bible decries laziness; it is scandalous and sinful. The writer of Proverbs has much to say about this (6:9–11; 10:5; 19:15; 21:25; 24:30–34), including the contrasting of the lazy with the diligent. "The hand of the diligent will rule, but the slack hand will be put to forced labor" (12:24). "The soul of the sluggard craves and gets nothing, but the soul of the diligent is made fat" (13:4; cf. 14:23). If you're diligent, you're likely to make money; if you're lazy, you probably won't.

The Book of Proverbs draws an example from the insect world to further admonish the lazy person and underscore the value of hard work: "Go to the ant, O sluggard, observe her ways and be wise, which, having no chief, officer or ruler, prepares her food in the summer and gathers her provision in the harvest" (6:6–8). The ant, without someone telling it what to do, uses its God-given instinct to gather food in the summer so it will have what it needs during the winter. On the other hand, intelligent but lazy human beings sometimes won't behave as prudently as the ant. Proverbs 20:4 says, "The sluggard does not plow after the autumn, so he begs during the harvest and has nothing." The lazy man does not work as hard as he should and therefore winds up a beggar.

The apostle Paul taught similar principles in the New Testament. He exhorted the believers in Thessalonica: "For even when we were with you, we used to give you this order: If anyone is not willing to work, then he is not to eat, either" (2 Thess. 3:10). He told Timothy to instruct church members on their work obligations: "If anyone does not provide for his own, and especially for those of his household, he has denied the faith and is worse than an unbeliever" (1 Tim. 5:8). If you do not work conscientiously and diligently to provide for your family, you're behaving worse than an unbeliever, because most non-Christians will at least work hard to care for their families.

We should be motivated to shun laziness because work is a noble endeavor, which should be performed to please the Lord (Col. 3:22–24). People often ask me, concerning my work as a pastor, "What sustains you? What keeps you going?" I tell them that I stay motivated because I work for the Lord. Everything I do is a service rendered to Him—and He evaluates it all. That's also true of any other job, whether you're flipping hamburgers, working in a warehouse, working as a machinist in a factory, teaching school, selling insurance, serving in law enforcement, writing computer software, or practicing medicine. That we are to work "not by way of eyeservice, as men-pleasers, but as slaves of Christ, doing the will of God from the heart" (Eph. 6:6) should be our elevating motivation as we strive to earn money that supports our families and provides additional wealth for the future.

Acquiring Money through Saving

Another God-honoring way to obtain money, especially with regard to our future well being, is to save it. Proverbs 21:20 says, "There is precious treasure and oil in the dwelling of the wise, but a foolish man swallows it up." A wise person lays aside some of his wealth ("treasure and oil") for the future and for unexpected times of need. The fool, however, spends all his income and unnecessarily lives paycheck to paycheck. A paraphrase of verse 20 really brings the issue into sharp focus: "The wise man saves for the future, but the foolish man spends whatever he gets" (TLB). To operate that way is absolutely foolish; you *need* to set some money aside for the future.

The ants in Proverbs again illustrate the point of saving: "The ants are not a strong people, but they prepare their food in the summer" (30:25). This implies that the ants know winter is coming each year and that they set aside extra from their summer food preparation. That is called saving for the future. You should save so you can accommodate yourself for a time when you're not able to work, or at least no longer able to earn as much money as you now do.

You also need to save for the unexpected. Circumstances arise from time to time—such as major injuries and illnesses, job losses, and natural disasters—that can have catastrophic effects in your life if you're not financially prepared. Special times also arise when you may want to give money to someone in serious need, assist your children as they get started in life, or contribute to some ministry effort. You will be able to give little or nothing if you have not saved or prepared for such contingencies.

One key component of saving money, and an important way to prepare for future needs, is to invest. Toward the end of the parable of the talents, which illustrates the tragedy of wasted opportunity, Jesus said, "Then you ought to have put my money in the bank, and on my arrival I would have received my money back with interest" (Matt. 25:27). He affirmed the value of using your money to earn money. If you have extra money, you should be faithful at least to put it into a savings account to earn interest. Better yet, as you are able, you should seize opportunities to increase your wealth through investments like certificates of deposit, money market accounts, mutual funds, individual stock and bond funds, and agricultural commodities. The Lord is pleased if you and I can be faithful in making wise financial investments, however, we also need to be sure to continually ask for His guidance as we do.

It is possible, however, to become obsessed with saving money. You can attempt to save at such a high level that you become a tightwad—extremely selfish and miserly with your funds, fearing that if you don't hold tightly to every penny now, you won't have enough to sustain your current lifestyle in the future. Such a mindset turns saving into hoarding and causes you to stop entrusting your financial future to God's control. And that's obviously not His will.

It is His will, however, that we save money. If done in a careful, thoughtful, balanced way—using legitimate means such as long-term savings, solid investments, individual retirement accounts, and the like—it is reasonable and biblical. Above all, God will be pleased.

Acquiring Money through Planning

If you're going to earn enough money to meet your obligations and save enough to have something for the future, it's essential that you plan (cf. Prov. 27:23–24). That may mean you need to stick to a carefully crafted budget. Or it may mean simply outlining a set of spending priorities and operating faithfully within those boundaries. Whichever way you do it, it's crucial not to spend more than you take in. That just makes good sense. Otherwise, you will not be a good financial steward and be able to save for future needs and emergencies.

If you are ever going to be a wise planner of your personal finances, you absolutely must ask yourself these questions: *Am I really exercising some form of carefully thought-out financial self-control? Or do I merely spend money carelessly and impulsively, with little or no regard for the future implications?* If the second question describes you, you might one day find yourself in a financial emergency, begging God to rescue you from a situation that, with better planning, you could have handled in a calmer way. Beware of losing financial self-control, and pray as David did, "Also, keep back Your servant from presumptuous sins; let them not rule over me" (Ps. 19:13).

For a number of reasons, today's Western culture makes it harder than ever for people to maintain good financial self-control. First, we are bombarded with more sophisticated advertising and marketing appeals. Local television stations, networks, and cable channels increasingly operate just for the commercial revenue. That's what pays for the programs we watch, even on public television. Advertisers have to recover what they pay for television commercials, therefore they work hard to get you to buy their product. The networks use commercial money to pay for programming, so they hope the advertisers will prosper and be able to afford increased commercial rates. It's all a huge scheme to get you to purchase more and more of what's advertised over the airwaves. Likewise, radio uses its programming to attract you to the many commercials it airs.

Newspapers, also, are more and more dependent on advertising for revenue. It's astounding how many pages in a typical American daily newspaper are now devoted to nothing but advertising—everything from department store ads for all sorts of items, ads for electronics, ads for cars and trucks, ads for alcoholic beverages, ads for fitness centers and athletic products. All of this has one big target audience in mind—you and me, the consumers.

Second, modern culture overemphasizes image. Advertisers seek to sell products by stressing that there's a certain fashionable and preferred image attached to where you live, what you drive, and what you wear. You never see car commercials that focus primarily on the quality of the car's basic features, or its safety and reliability as a mode of transportation. Instead, such television commercials will typically feature a beautiful woman driving the car, some pulsating theme music, and a quick sequence of film showing the car roaring down a scenic country or mountain road. You usually get a distorted picture of the car's actual appearance and very little information about the car itself. In fact, car commercials will often give you more information about the price and financing of the car than about the car's features. The main concerns are image and getting you to buy the product.

I'm not saying we shouldn't enjoy life's good things, such as comfortable, well-engineered cars. But I am pointing out that advertisers, in selling big-ticket items like cars, emphasize style and glitz over substance and reality. We need to be careful and discerning lest such commercials tempt us to buy things we don't need or can't afford.

Another modern reality that makes all those appeals work and severely challenges people's efforts at financial self-control is the credit card. With only minimal credit worthiness, individuals can obtain plastic charge cards and use them to buy almost anything. For most goods and services, you no longer need to pay the total cost up front—or even put any money down—to get what you want. You merely put the purchase price on your credit card's account and worry later about paying off the balance with high interest.

In just the past decade, the total credit card debt in the

United States has become enormous. In 1994 it was approximately 525 billion dollars, accompanied by an average annual interest rate of 18 percent. Today the total is probably much closer to one trillion dollars. And it is estimated that 70 percent of credit card holders carry large balances on their cards—balances that earn banks and other card issuers close to two hundred million dollars daily in total interest income.

Credit card experts say that once the average cardholder becomes eight hundred dollars or more in debt to his credit card company, the company has him or her for life. Most people can't pay off an eight hundred-dollar debt because they live at the level of their income. And eight hundred dollars is not even half the average amount of credit card debt in U.S. households. The typical American owes more than two thousand dollars at the high interest rate of 18 percent. If you're in that position, you're in financial bondage to your credit card company. Proverbs 22:7 characterizes this situation accurately: "The rich rules over the poor, and the borrower becomes the lender's slave."

Merchants almost encourage the credit card debt predicament by readily accepting cards. Studies show that you spend as much as 80 percent more using a credit card than you do using a check or cash. Merchants want to exploit that tendency; for them, taking credit cards is a smart way of doing business. The process is convenient and quick, and before you know it, the debt balance on your various cards is much greater than you ever expected.[2]

The Lord, on the other hand, wants you to plan well enough so you're not paying off huge sums of high-interest debt to your credit card company. Paul reminded the Corinthians, "You were bought with a price; do not become slaves of men" (1 Cor. 7:23). If you exercise self-control and use your credit card with restraint (or not at all), you'll be able to give more to the Lord and set aside more money for savings, investments, and wiser spending opportunities.

Finally, careful planning will help you avoid the pitfalls of loaning money to other people. Unless you have studied a certain opportunity to loan money and concluded that it would be an excellent and wise investment, be cautious about giving other people control over your resources. (I would exclude from this caution those occasional opportunities you might have to help a close member of your family. For example, helping a child buy a house or car.) Proverbs again gives us practical advice, "A man lacking in sense pledges and becomes guarantor in the presence of his neighbor" (17:18). Becoming a guarantor simply means you're countersigning for someone else to borrow money, and you make yourself liable for that person's entire debt if he cannot repay it. You have not made a direct loan to him, but you have potentially relinquished control of your God-given resources to his financial irresponsibility and lack of good judgment. Scripture says it's unwise to do that—you're placing yourself in a very precarious position. Therefore, don't countersign for a friend or neighbor's debt.

God has entrusted every Christian with a stewardship of money and possessions. Every last cent of our money and the smallest items of our material possessions belong to Him. Therefore we must use all of our resources for God's honor and glory. That includes enjoying the wonderful creation He has given us, working diligently to provide for the basic needs of our families, saving and investing for the future, and planning carefully so we wisely exercise financial self-control.

Good stewardship will be motivated by what Christ said concerning the relationship of how we use our money and our spiritual fruitfulness. "He who is faithful in a very little thing is faithful also in much; and he who is unrighteous in a very little thing is unrighteous also in much. Therefore if you have not been faithful in the use of unrighteous wealth, who will entrust the true riches to you?" (Luke 16:10–11). Christ is saying that God will not give you a fruitful spiritual ministry in the lives of people ("the true riches") if you don't learn how to handle money.

Thus, if you want the Lord to use you in the advancement of His kingdom, you have a great incentive to be a good steward of the wealth He has bestowed on you. How you handle money and possessions is crucial—it's a barometer of your Christian life and a test of how well you understand that the true riches are spiritual. A more detailed understanding of where the ultimate riches lie is the theme of the next chapter.

"Do not store up for yourselves treasures on earth, where moth and rust destroy, and where thieves break in and steal. But store up for yourselves treasures in heaven, where neither moth nor rust destroys, and where thieves do not break in or steal; for where your treasure is, there your heart will be also."

—Matthew 6:19–21

4   Our True Riches Are in Heaven

NO MATTER HOW MUCH teaching we receive concerning the nature of money, the need to avoid undue love of it, the proper ways to acquire it, and the freedom to enjoy God's rich creation, we must constantly strive to maintain scriptural, Christ-centered perspective regarding material and spiritual prosperity. The apostle Paul's command to "set your mind on the things above, not on the things that are on the earth" (Col. 3:2) ought to stimulate constant reminders to thwart the relentless temptations around and in us.

However, as we suggested in the previous chapter, so many forces in today's fast-paced, high-tech, consumer-oriented society wage a relentless war against a biblical perspective on money and possessions. The ultimate goal in the world's eyes seems to be for people to place supreme confidence in prosperity itself and their abilities to manipulate its tools to their own advantage. But that goal in many ways simply reflects the attitudes people had seventy years ago, at a crucial turning point in American history. Historian Frederick Lewis Allen portrayed Americans' view of the good economic times in the summer of 1929:

On every side one heard the new wisdom sagely expressed. "Prosperity due for a decline? Why, man, we've scarcely started!" "Be a bull on America." "Never sell the United States short." "I tell you, some of these prices will look ridiculously low in another year or two." "Just watch that stock—it's going to five hundred." "The possibilities of that company are *unlimited.*" "Never give up your position in a good stock." Everybody heard how many millions a man would have made if he had bought a hundred shares of General Motors in 1919 and held on. Everybody was reminded at some time or another that George F. Baker never sold anything. As for the menace of speculation, one was glibly assured that—as Ex-Governor Stokes of New Jersey had proclaimed in an eloquent speech—Columbus, Washington, Franklin, and Edison had all been speculators. "The way of wealth," wrote John J. Raskob in an article in the *Ladies Home Journal* alluringly titled "Everybody Ought to Be Rich," "is to get into the profit end of wealth production in this country," and he pointed out that if one saved but fifteen dollars a month and invested it in good common stocks, allowing the dividends and rights to accumulate, at the end of twenty years one would have at least eighty thousand dollars and an income from investments of at least four hundred dollars a month. It was all so easy. The gateway to fortune stood wide open.[1]

In the fall of 1929 the same stock market that people had touted so highly in the summer, and indeed for much of the previous decade, collapsed and ushered in the worst economic depression in American history. While there are many differences between the economic good times of the 1920s and the prosperous times in America at the end of the century—respected economic observers rarely say that today's bull market will suffer the same fate as the 1929 stock market—the point is simply this: Prosperity is still very uncertain. We dare not make it the basis of our spiritual security. God in His sovereignty may decide at any time, as with Job, to test us by removing our money, possessions, and even family members.

Although there is a definite relationship between spiritual fruitfulness and how well we handle our wealth (cf. Luke 16:10–11), the Lord does not want us to misunderstand that connection and thereby make wrong and sinful assumptions. Throughout redemptive history, false religious teachers—such as the scribes and Pharisees—have twisted the relationship between money and spirituality. Instead of adhering to the biblical prescription that says fiscal responsibility gives believers the opportunity to be blessed with spiritual ministry, false teachers have taught that material blessing results from spiritual superiority. "If we are rich in this world's goods, it must mean God is pleased with us and doesn't mind if we concentrate all our energies on accumulating more wealth." This is really just an extended definition of today's prosperity gospel, and could not be more wrong or unscriptural.

Such teaching turns upside down passages like Deuteronomy 28:1–3, "Now it shall be, if you diligently obey the LORD your God, being careful to do all His commandments which I command you today, the LORD your God will set you high above all the nations of the earth. All these blessings will come upon you and overtake you, if you obey the LORD your God. Blessed shall you be in the city, and blessed shall you be in the country." The blessings Moses spoke of are unmistakably contingent on obedience to God. You are not reflecting His blessing and approval if you amass material luxuries and extra money by greedily and selfishly becoming preoccupied with such endeavors (cf. Prov. 23:4).

To claim the Lord's approval merely on the basis of your personal prosperity and comfort is to dishonor His name and badly misinterpret His Word.

Mainly in response to the Pharisees' erroneous teachings and sinful practices concerning wealth (cf. Matt. 23:1–7, 25–28; Luke 16:14–15), Jesus in the Sermon on the Mount taught His disciples to have a correct perspective on wealth and possessions:

> Do not store up for yourselves treasures on earth, where moth and rust destroy, and where thieves break in and steal. But store up for yourselves treasures in heaven, where neither moth nor rust destroys, and where thieves do not break in or steal; for where your treasure is, there your heart will be also. The eye is the lamp of the body; so then if your eye is clear, your whole body will be full of light. But if your eye is bad, your whole body will be full of darkness. If then the light that is in you is darkness, how great is the darkness! No one can serve two masters; for either he will hate the one and love the other, or he will be devoted to one and despise the other. You cannot serve God and wealth. (Matt. 6:19–24)

Here Jesus exhorts us to have a single treasure, a single vision, and a single master whenever we consider our material blessings.

HAVING A SINGLE TREASURE

The key warning in Jesus' opening statement (v. 19) is that we do not accumulate finances and material goods simply for our own satisfaction. If we do that, possessions become idols. The original wording for "do not store up" connotes a laying out horizontally, as one stacks coins. In this context Jesus is using the phrase to prohibit hoarding or any form of unwise stockpiling. It pictures wealth that is simply stored for safe-keeping and not used. A person who does that is usually eager to show off his riches or portray an image of comfortable indulgence (cf. Luke 12:16–21).

On the contrary, we are cheerfully, wisely, and generously to use our possessions in support of and to further God's kingdom. In doing so, we'll gain heavenly wealth and not be hindered by the stumblingblocks of unused money and goods. In addition, such idle possessions sooner or later begin to deteriorate. And even if we could perfectly protect our wealth from theft, destruction, or even boredom, we ultimately lose possession of it at our death. But when we use all the resources God has bestowed on us, whether money and property, or time and energy and ideas, to honor God, provide for family, and minister to others, that generates heavenly resources that nothing on earth can destroy or steal. Heavenly security provides the only absolute safeguard for our treasures.

Christ goes on to tell all who follow Him that "where your treasure is, there your heart will be also" (Matt. 6:21). Your most beloved possessions are inseparably linked to your strongest motives, priorities, and desires. It is impossible for the true Christian to have his treasures anchored to the world if his heart is fixed on heaven (cf. 1 John 2:15–16).

If your heart is right concerning your wealth, then you will willingly invest money in God's kingdom. But if you are reluctant to give God your resources—and you continually display attitudes of self-indulgence, stinginess, and covetousness—you need to reexamine your relationship to the Lord.

Christ was not telling the disciples that if they spent their riches for spiritual purposes their hearts would automatically become right with Him. But He was saying that how we spend our wealth indicates the *existing* spiritual condition of our heart. If your attitude toward the use of money reveals an unrighteous heart, turn to the Book of Nehemiah and follow the pattern of God's people. After returning from exile in Babylon, the Jews returned to God's Word and a revival began. "Ezra opened the book in the sight of all the people" and various leaders took turns reading "from the law of God" (Neh. 8:5–8). The power of Scripture convicted them of their sin, caused them to turn to obedience and faithfulness in support of God's work, and resulted in praise to Him (chaps. 9–10).

One's attitude toward money and possessions is a vital concern to God, and any genuine work of the Spirit will affect that attitude in a positive way. When Israel built the tabernacle, "everyone whose heart stirred him and everyone whose spirit moved him came and brought the Lord's contribution for the work of the tent of meeting and for all its service and for the holy garments" (Exod. 35:21). King David gave generously toward the building of the temple, and "the rulers of the fathers' households, and the princes of the tribes of Israel, and the commanders of thousands and of hundreds, with the overseers over the king's work, offered willingly. . . . Then the people rejoiced because they had offered so willingly, for they made their offering to the Lord with a whole heart, and King David also rejoiced greatly" (1 Chron. 29:2–6, 9).

The biblical principle for believers has always been, "Honor the Lord from your wealth and from the first of all your produce; so your barns will be filled with plenty and your vats will overflow with new wine" (Prov. 3:9–10). Christ taught, "Give, and it will be given to you. They will pour into your lap a good measure—pressed down, shaken together, and running over. For by your standard of measure it will be measured to you in return" (Luke 6:38). Similarly, the apostle Paul wrote, "he who sows sparingly will also reap sparingly, and he who sows bountifully will also reap bountifully" (2 Cor. 9:6). Generosity has always been God's formula for acquiring permanent and guaranteed spiritual dividends—and they always result when we have our primary treasure in heaven (cf. Luke 16:9).

HAVING A SINGLE VISION

In Matthew 6:22–23, Jesus elaborates on His illustration of the heart and basically calls it the eye of the soul: "The eye is the lamp of the body; so then if your eye is clear, your whole body will be full of light. But if your eye is bad, your whole body will be full of darkness. If then the light that is in you is darkness, how great is the darkness!" The eye is the body's only channel of light, and therefore the only means of vision. Likewise, the heart (mind) is the soul's only channel through which spiritual realities shine. Through it we receive God's truth, love, peace, and every other kind of spiritual blessing. Therefore it is essential that you keep your heart, or spiritual eye, clear and properly focused.

The King James translation renders the Greek for "clear" as "single," referring to a heart that has singleness of purpose and is devoted to what's right—regarding resources as well as every other aspect of the Christian life. As J. C. Ryle said more than a century ago, "Singleness of purpose is one great secret of spiritual prosperity."

A "bad eye," one that is damaged because of disease or injury, stands in contrast to that clarity and singleness of purpose. It does not allow light to enter and leaves the whole body full of darkness. If our hearts become weighed down and preoccupied with material concerns, they become blind and insensitive to spiritual concerns—"full of darkness."

According to Jesus' illustration, a "bad eye" equals a self-ish and indulgent heart. Such a heart is self-deceived and cannot recognize true light. What it thinks is light is actually darkness, and Jesus emphasized how tragic that condition is when He exclaimed "how great is the darkness!"

So by simple and sobering comparisons, Jesus presents the principle we have already seen: the way we view money and how we spend it are sure measurements of our true spiritual condition.

HAVING A SINGLE MASTER

Jesus concludes His teaching in this passage on the right perspective toward material possessions with a clear command about our allegiance: "No one can serve two masters; for either he will hate the one and love the other, or he will be devoted to one and despise the other. You cannot serve God and wealth" (Matt. 6:24).

The Greek word for "masters" (*kurios;* sometimes translated "lord") refers to one who owns and oversees slaves. Thus "masters" means more than the simple concept of employer, of which we may have more than one and work acceptably for each during the same week or month. This command, therefore, is not against the modern practice of working two or more jobs and fulfilling one's obligation to several employers.

A slave owed his full-time service and allegiance to a single master. The master totally owned and controlled the slave, so that the slave was not supposed to have anything left to give to anyone else. It was not only difficult but also impossible to serve two masters and render full and faithful obedience to each one.

Jesus affirmed the truth, which Paul and other New Testament writers would articulate many times, that He was

Lord and Master over His followers, who were the willing bondslaves. Romans 6 explains that prior to salvation you and I were enslaved to our master, sin. But when we embraced Jesus' saving work, we became slaves of God and His righteous commands (vv. 16–22).

We can't claim Christ as Lord if we serve any other master—wealth, our job, other people, ourselves—than Him. If we know what God's Word says about the right perspective toward and proper use of money, but don't follow those teachings, we demonstrate that our allegiance is not fully to Christ. "Where riches hold the dominion of the heart," John Calvin wrote, "God has lost His authority."

Concerning wealth, God through His Son Jesus Christ makes a clear-cut distinction: Your treasure is either on earth or in heaven; your master is either God or money and earthly goods. The orders of those two masters are completely incompatible. One says walk by faith, but the other demands that you walk by sight. One urges you to be humble, but the other tempts you to be proud. Christ the Master calls you to set your mind on things above, but the master that is wealth and materialism would lead you to focus on things below.

If you have acknowledged Christ as your Master, you will readily agree with the apostle Paul's admonition: "Whether, then, you eat or drink or whatever you do, do all to the glory of God" (1 Cor. 10:31). G. Campbell Morgan had several insightful observations about the believer's real identity and the temporality of his money and possessions that all Christians should embrace regarding their treasures:

> You are to remember with the passion burning within you that you are not the child of today. You are not of the earth, you are more than dust; you are the child of tomorrow, you are of the eternities, you are the offspring of Deity. The measurements of

your lives cannot be circumscribed by the point where blue sky kisses green earth. All the fact of your life cannot be encompassed in the one small sphere upon which you live. You belong to the infinite. If you make your fortune on the earth— poor, sorry, silly soul—you have made a fortune, and stored it in a place where you cannot hold it. Make your fortune, but store it where it will greet you in the dawning of the new morning.[2]

"Remember the words of the Lord Jesus, that He Himself said, 'It is more blessed to give than to receive.'"

—Acts 20:35

5   The Biblical Model for Giving

CHRISTIANS EXPRESS ALL SORTS OF PREFERENCES for why they most look forward to coming to church on the Lord's Day. On any given week that reason may be less than spiritual and noble. One might be eager to discuss a business deal with a fellow member. He might want to show off a new suit of clothes that he purchased at a bargain, or he might want to make a fashion statement. Or he might want to tell people in his Sunday school class all about his family's recent vacation. Those obviously are not biblical reasons for being eager about attending worship services.

But even among the scriptural, godly reasons for anticipating weekly worship at your local church—the preaching of Scripture, the worshipful music and praise during the service, the quality fellowship and mutual ministry opportunities— there is one that rarely tops the list. I'm convinced that if we really understood the Scriptures and what God has promised in them, we would most look forward to each Lord's day at church because of *the weekly offering.* That conclusion may strike you as strange. But, according to the Word, your opportunity to participate in the weekly offering results in a direct pipeline to spiritual blessing. In fact, if you look at only two of Jesus' statements out of all the other verses about giving, those two alone should convince you to anticipate the offering more than any other element of the worship service. And His words ought to prompt you to be generous and sacrificial every time you give.

TWO DEFINING STATEMENTS

Luke's account of the Sermon on the Mount contains the first of Jesus' two key statements on the benefits of giving: "Give, and it will be given to you. They will pour into your lap a good measure—pressed down, shaken together, and running over. For by your standard of measure it will be measured to you in return" (Luke 6:38).

Our Lord used symbolism derived from the Middle Eastern grain market of His day. When men and women went to the market they would pull up a large portion of their long flowing robe through their belt and use both hands to form a basket-like pocket. The grain dealer would then pour the purchased amount of grain into the person's lap— into that huge pocket they had formed with their garment.

That concept is specifically mentioned in Ruth 3:15, "'Give me the cloak that is on you and hold it.' So she held it, and he measured six measures of barley and laid it on her. Then she went into the city." The prophet Malachi saw a much larger expansion of such individual giving when he commanded the nation: "'Bring the whole tithe into the storehouse, so that there may be food in My house, and test Me now in this,' says the LORD of hosts, 'if I will not open for you the windows of heaven and pour out for you a blessing until it overflows'" (Mal. 3:10).

However, Jesus was not merely making a passing reference

to an Old Testament precept. As part of His discourse on principles for living in God's kingdom, He was making it a New Testament principle. The apostle Paul confirms this by expressing the standard in different words, but with equal force: "He who sows sparingly will also reap sparingly, and he who sows bountifully will also reap bountifully" (2 Cor. 9:6). The underlying truth is simply this: Generosity in giving results in a greater reward from God.

Paul, in his farewell exhortation to the Ephesian elders, further reinforces the New Covenant validity of the principle by quoting another statement from Jesus: "Remember the words of the Lord Jesus, that He Himself said, 'It is more blessed to give than to receive'" (Acts 20:35). That is the only recorded earthly statement of Jesus outside the four Gospels (excluding the statements in the Book of Revelation spoken by the glorified Christ). That underscores and enhances the priority of the principle of giving. Out of Jesus' many unrecorded words (cf. John 21:25), the Holy Spirit chose to include only that short statement about the blessings of giving.

Those two monumental promises from Jesus should be all we need to make us welcome with joy every giving opportunity. They ought to motivate you and me—whether it's through the weekly offering at church or meeting someone's individual need—always to give as generously, unselfishly, and sacrificially as possible.

But sadly many professed Christians don't seem to realize that Jesus' two promises make giving a matter of faith and obedience. They cling to the notion that they must protect their assets and hang on to everything they own. Instead, they should be trusting the promises of God's Word and giving with a generous spirit. In Luke 6:38, the Greek for "give" is in the imperative, which makes it a command from Jesus that must be obeyed. Giving is therefore an issue of believing His command and following through in faithful obedience. If you do, you demonstrate your trust in His promises. If you don't, you sin against Christ in the sense that you have no faith in what He promised about the blessings of giving.

THE JERUSALEM CHURCH: A CASE STUDY IN GIVING

From its inception, the early church obeyed Jesus' commands concerning the grace of giving. First of all, the members' gifts supported the church's leaders—the apostles, prophets, evangelists, and pastors. Paul advocated the validity of such support:

> Or do only Barnabas and I not have a right to refrain from working? Who at any time serves as a soldier at his own expense? Who plants a vineyard and does not eat the fruit of it? Or who tends a flock and does not use the milk of the flock? I am not speaking these things according to human judgment, am I? Or does not the Law also say these things? For it is written in the Law of Moses, "You shall not muzzle the ox while he is threshing." God is not concerned about oxen, is He? Or is He speaking altogether for our sake? Yes, for our sake it was written, because the plowman ought to plow in hope, and the thresher to thresh in hope of sharing the crops. If we sowed spiritual things in you, is it too much if we reap material things from you? (1 Cor. 9:6–11)

Certain work, including that of ones who minister full-time in leading the church, inherently requires financial compensation. Therefore God commands us to give for the support of those whom He sends to serve us, teach us, and lead us in the church (1 Cor. 9:14; Gal. 6:6; 1 Tim. 5:17).

The second way in which the early church directed its giving—to the needs of the general church population—is an excellent model of how we ought to care for the neediest of fellow believers in our midst. The church at Jerusalem highlights the necessity for such a ministry because from the Day of Pentecost it was filled with poor and needy people—widows, orphans, and folks with generally meager resources. The New Testament and secular history reveal the main causes for that situation and how the church responded to it.

A Church of Pilgrims

The Jerusalem church was an impoverished congregation because it contained many spiritual pilgrims. They were Jews who had come to Jerusalem from every part of Israel and all over the Gentile (Hellenistic) world (Acts 2:9–11) for the celebration of Pentecost, the Jewish religious feast that occurred forty days after Passover.

On that particular Pentecost day, following the ascension of Christ, the Holy Spirit gave miraculous birth to the church (see Acts 2) as three thousand converts joined the one hundred twenty who already believed. The Jerusalem church was then the only local assembly in the world where Christians could have fellowship and grow in their faith. With all the joyful, euphoric excitement generated when they witnessed daily miracles by the apostles, the hundreds of enthusiastic pilgrim converts had no desire or reason to return home.

At the beginning of their pilgrimage, prior to conversion, the Hellenistic Jews would have stayed in inns or with relatives. But neither of those situations could have lasted for very long. Those who stayed in inns would have run out of money, and those who were guests of Jewish relatives would have been evicted for converting to Christianity. The only alternative for most of the pilgrims was to stay with Jewish believers in and around Jerusalem.

The pilgrims who remained tended to be the poorer ones—the widows, the orphans, and those who had nothing to go home to. The smaller number that returned home were the ones who had an estate, who owned a business, who had a responsible government job somewhere—generally those who had more control over their own circumstances.

Therefore the relatively small band of Jewish believers in the Jerusalem church tried valiantly to take on the full support of several thousand converted pilgrims. But that was no easy task because the Jewish believers themselves were low-income people with modest housing facilities. The entire undertaking was made even more difficult and complicated by the special needs of the widows—the Jewish widows already there and those brought into the church from the influx of Hellenistic pilgrims. The church leaders chose seven faithful and godly men to locate all the Hellenistic widows, and to make sure they were included in the daily food allocation (Acts 6:1–7). As part of its ministry to the poor, the Jerusalem church had to purchase, prepare, and distribute food to all those widows.

Such circumstances previewed the principle that both Paul and James later wrote in their epistles to the early church. "For consider your calling, brethren, that there were not many wise according to the flesh, not many mighty, not many noble" (1 Cor. 1:26). "Listen, my beloved brethren: did not God choose the poor of this world to be rich in faith and heirs of the kingdom which He promised to those who love Him?" (James 2:5). The Lord has always had a special place in His heart for the poor and lowly (Deut. 15:7–11; Ps. 41:1–3; Prov. 14:31; 19:17; 21:13; 22:9), and He was pleased when the Jerusalem church ministered diligently to the needy in its midst.

A Church with Persecuted Jews

From the beginning the Jerusalem church also contained many persecuted Jewish believers, which is the second reason it was poor. In fact, the Jerusalem church was essentially a Jewish church, which means that almost the entire body of believers would have been one large group of persecuted Jews. That situation resulted from the devout, but unbelieving Jews' fierce loyalty to Judaism.

Those Jews, under the leadership of the scribes and Pharisees, had a legalistic, sectarian animosity toward any Jew who would reject Judaism and come to faith in Christ. Any convert to Christianity would be immediately ostracized from the Jewish community, just as he or she would be today under orthodox Judaism. That's what happened to the many new believers in the Jerusalem church in the days following Pentecost. They were hated by friends and disowned by family, excommunicated from the synagogue, and completely rejected by the community. They would lose their businesses or get fired from their jobs and thus lose their sources of income. Therefore, two downtrodden segments constituted the great majority of the Jerusalem church—the many pilgrim converts and now these dispossessed Jews.

Such persecution of Jewish believers was simply a fulfillment of what Jesus taught His disciples: "Remember the word that I said to you, 'A slave is not greater than his master.' If they persecuted Me, they will also persecute you" (John 15:20). And He also promised the disciples that many of them, on the way to inheriting eternal life, would lose family and possessions (Matt. 19:29; cf. John 16:2).

A Church under the Roman Economy

The economy of Jerusalem and the surrounding area was as poor as any economy in the Roman Empire. That situation was a third component contributing to the general poverty of the Jerusalem church.

As was true with all outlying territories of their empire, the Romans exacerbated the impoverishment of those living in Jerusalem by extracting all the valuable natural resources and importing whatever finished products they wanted from the area. Rome also overtaxed the people by hiring Jewish collectors to extort money from their own people. The Romans used that revenue to enrich their coffers and finance some of their grandiose projects.

Jerusalem's struggling economy was further strained by a worldwide famine, which was predicted by Agabus the prophet: "One of them named Agabus stood up and began to indicate by the Spirit that there would certainly be a great famine all over the world. And this took place in the reign of Claudius" (Acts 11:28).

The Jerusalem church, however, was undaunted in the face of all those extremely challenging odds. In spite of so much hardship and poverty, its members initially gave everything they could in an effort to obey Jesus' command that it is more blessed to give than receive.

A Church that Gave Its All

The Jerusalem church's effort to follow the principle that generosity in giving results in a greater reward from God was truly exceptional and noble. Acts 2:44–45 records what happened: "And all those who had believed were together and had all things in common; and they began selling their property and possessions and were sharing them with all, as anyone might have need." There was a unity and commonality in the fellowship, and people held possessions with an open hand, realizing that they owned everything for the common good of the church. Whoever needed something, could have it. The church's generosity ran deep—members understood that one cannot outgive God, so they sold what they had and gave to the poorer believers.

Acts 4:32–35 gives us additional commentary on the extraordinarily generous giving practices of the Jerusalem church, and the blessed results.

> The congregation of those who believed were of one heart and soul; and not one of them claimed that anything belonging to him was his own, but all things were common property to them. And with great power the apostles were giving testimony to the resurrection of the Lord Jesus, and abundant grace was upon them all. For there was not a needy person among them, for all who were owners of land or houses would sell them and bring the proceeds of the sales and lay them at the apostles' feet, and they would be distributed to each as any had need.

Those early Christians knew and believed the truth that everything belongs to God, and that all His resources are simply to be made available to those who need them most. That's the real meaning of the phrase "all things were common property to them" (v. 32). (It does not mean, as some have interpreted it, that the church divided and distributed all its money and possessions in a socialistic fashion, with everyone receiving an equal amount of wealth.)

That system worked well for the church at Jerusalem during its early years, but before long there was nothing left to sell and no more money to distribute. The people in the church had courageously given their all, and now the apostle Paul and others began viewing them not as those who could continue to give, but as those who urgently needed the help of other believers.

"NOW CONCERNING THE COLLECTION"

As the original apostles (Peter, James, and John) validated Paul's early ministry, they taught him to have a heartfelt concern for poor believers: "They only asked us to remember the poor—the very thing I also was eager to do" (Gal. 2:10; cf. 2 Cor. 6:10). Paul dearly loved the impoverished saints in Jerusalem as brothers and sisters in Christ and knew God wanted their needs met. He saw that they would not be able to sustain themselves in the face of increasing persecution and in view of the ongoing needs of the pilgrims and widows. Therefore Paul made the needs of the Jerusalem church the object of a special offering project.

The project was first referred to generally in Acts 11:29–30, "And in the proportion that any of the disciples had means, each of them determined to send a contribution for the relief of the brethren living in Judea. And this they did, sending it in charge of Barnabas and Saul to the elders." That effort became a high priority for Paul during his third missionary journey (cf. Acts 18:23–21:16).

Paul gives us the first detailed, recorded teaching concerning his great relief project for the Jerusalem church in 1 Corinthians 16:1–4,

Now concerning the collection for the saints, as I directed the churches of Galatia, so do you also. On the first day of every week each one of you is to put aside and save, as he may prosper, so that no collections be made when I come. When I arrive, whomever you may approve, I will send them with letters to carry your gift to Jerusalem; and if it is fitting for me to go also, they will go with me.

This passage contains several important principles on giving that not only explain how Paul wanted that specific collection conducted, but also indicate what kind of model for Christian giving the church today ought to follow.

When Should We Give?

First of all, Paul says the most fitting time for Christian giving is weekly, during the public worship. Paul's reference to the first day of the week indicates that the early worship services included a regular offering. It is also a strong indicator that our giving should be consistent and systematic, not spasmodic and subjective ("as the Spirit leads"), or whenever we happen to remember it. Obviously, the Holy Spirit can sometimes prompt us to give in response to special appeals for urgent needs. However, as in every other major aspect of the Christian life, the Spirit uses scriptural instructions like Paul's to guide our giving.

The apostle's guidelines are not rigid, requiring that people divide their offering money so they always have something to put into the plate or basket each Sunday. It may work better for them to give just once a month, if they are paid monthly, or less frequently than that, if they are paid periodically as a commissioned salesperson or freelance worker. The point is simply this: You should be consistently aware of and responsive to the needs of your church (which includes budgeting ahead of everything else how much you will give to the Lord), even when you don't have anything to give on a particular Sunday. The offering is a required part of weekly worship and fellowship, one of your Christian responsibilities in lifting up "spiritual sacrifices" to God (1 Pet. 2:5).

Is Anybody Exempt from Giving?

Paul's directive to the Corinthian church, "each one of you" (1 Cor. 16:2) is universal in eliminating any excuse and not exempting any believer from the regular ministry of giving. God has made all His children stewards over a certain amount of wealth, even if it is small. He commands all to be generous with whatever they have, just as the widow with the two coins was (Mark 12:41–44).

If you are affluent, you can afford to give much before it even touches your lifestyle—and you should give sacrificially, so that it does limit your self-indulgence, unlike the rich donors who preceded the widow at the temple treasury (v. 44). Though it is not easy to give much when you have a low income, that should not be an excuse for giving nothing. So whether you are rich or poor, if you are a believer you should be openhanded and give in proportion to what you have. If you start out by being generous when you have modest resources, you will much more likely be generous when you have greater wealth (cf. Luke 16:10).

How Should We Give?

In 1 Corinthians 16:2, Paul goes on to tell the Corinthian believers, and us, how we should give through the church. When he writes that everyone should "put aside and save" he literally means "each one of you by himself lay up, or store up." The Greek word for "put aside and save" is a verb form of a term from which we get *thesaurus* (collection, treasury of words). It represents a chest or storehouse of some kind where money and valuables were kept. In New Testament times, such treasuries were part of the religious temples and were repositories for people's cash and valuables as well as their gifts to the temple. Paul's usage in verse 2 suggests that church members were to put aside money in a church repository designated for offerings.

The reason Paul gave his instructions the way he did ("that no collections be made when I come") was simply for the sake of efficiency. He wanted the Corinthians to have their large offering ready for him to take with him to Jerusalem when he arrived. Otherwise the church would have had to gather the money in a hurry after Paul arrived and, no doubt, the amount would have been far less than that accumulated over many months. But that directive does not rule out having a private offering fund set aside at home so that we may have money available to meet the emergency needs of others more directly and privately, as opportunities arise.

How Much Should We Give?

The biblical model does not mandate a certain amount or proportion of what we ought to give. Instead, the apostle Paul says believers have complete discretion to give as God prospers them. That disproves the claim among some Christians that says believers should give at least 10 percent of their income to the Lord's work, just as the ancient Israelites had to. (We will look at this question of the tithe in detail in chapter 7.)

In some ways your giving corresponds only generally to the Old Testament pattern. You give tax payments to support the government (Rom. 13:6), just as the Jews gave tithes to support their leadership (Lev. 27:30; Num. 18:21; Deut. 14:28–29; cf. Matt. 17:24–27; 22:15–21). In attitude, however, there is a direct parallel. You are to decide with joy what to give (2 Cor. 9:7), just as the Israelites gave from the heart (Exod. 25:1–2; 36:5–6; cf. 2 Sam. 24:24). God is always pleased when His people follow those basic guidelines of proportional and sacrificial giving.

How Should We Protect What's Given?

It is all right for you to expect your offering monies to be used properly and for the purposes given. To that end, Paul gave instruction to the Corinthian church: "When I arrive, whomever you may approve, I will send them with letters to carry your gift to Jerusalem" (1 Cor. 16:3). Your church should also entrust its financial matters to godly and responsible men. When the apostles first recognized the need in the Jerusalem church, their primary concern was to select men who had impeccable moral and spiritual qualifications (Acts 6:2–3). Such men will prayerfully oversee the use and investment of the offerings, as good stewards who present your monies before the Lord.

The opening verses of 1 Corinthians 16 present the essential model for how Christian giving should be handled. Paul encourages the Corinthian believers and those of any era to give freely and lovingly, with heartfelt concern. He knew that one of the surest indicators of genuine conversion is a man or woman's willingness to give generously whenever the opportunity arises, whether that be weekly or on special occasions: "But whoever has the world's goods, and sees his brother in need and closes his heart against him, how does the love of God abide in him?" (1 John 3:17).

6

"So let each one give as he purposes in his heart, not grudgingly or of necessity; for God loves a cheerful giver."

—2 Corinthians 9:7

6 *The Characteristics of Biblical Giving*

WORLD WAR II was the most devastating conflict in history, causing the death of millions of people, especially in Europe. At the close of the war the Allies, as part of their effort to rebuild Europe, assumed the care of millions of orphans from cities all over the continent. Relief officials built various camps to care for those children. As the program developed, the capacity of the camps had to be expanded because of the vast number of children that were being found and brought to the facilities. The orphans received the best care available, including the healthiest of food and drink.

But the administrators at one of the camps became very disturbed because the children, after just a few weeks, were no longer sleeping. Even though they received three meals a day, were clothed and bathed, and had adequate beds to sleep in, the children began staying awake all night. The perplexed officials interviewed the boys and girls as part of a study to discover the source of the problem. Before long they found a solution and implemented it.

The dormitory attendants began placing a small loaf of bread into the hand of each little child at bedtime. So before falling asleep the last thing each boy or girl would experience was the feel of bread in their hand. In a matter of days the children were all sleeping through the night, reassured by the bread that there would be food for tomorrow. They had been anxious because past experience had taught them that having food one day didn't necessarily guarantee anything for the next. But when they began to fall asleep with a small loaf in one hand, their fear was dispelled.

Philippians 4:19 is the loaf of bread God places into your hand each day: "And my God will supply all your needs according to His riches in glory in Christ Jesus." You have no reason to fear tomorrow because God will meet all your needs, and that should have a very positive effect on how you give. While you ought to plan wisely and save prudently for the future, you should also remember that you are not alone in securing your future. If God were to ask you to take your savings and invest them in His kingdom, you should be able to confidently obey Him, knowing that He will replace what you gave.

Paul introduced the church at Corinth to a group of believers who lived with a Philippians 4:19 confidence (2 Cor. 8). They were the Macedonian churches, whose example provides us with many God-centered principles for giving. The Macedonians characterize biblical giving because they understood the promises of God, and thus were so secure in their hope of the future that they willingly gave toward the present-day needs of others.

The exemplary churches of Macedonia were located in the cities of Philippi, Berea, and Thessalonica in the northern part of Greece. They were geographically close to the church at Corinth in the south, but they resided in the midst of far different circumstances. Macedonia, a Roman province for the previous two hundred years, had its economy harshly plundered by the Romans. That, along with a series of wars, had reduced the region to extreme impoverishment.

In addition to being located in the middle of such oppressive poverty, the Macedonian churches had endured a lot of persecution. In spite of their poverty, they were willing to give what they had in order to help other impoverished churches (Jerusalem).

Paul praises the Macedonians' generosity as he continues to instruct and encourage the Corinthians, and us, regarding the virtues of giving. The characteristics of biblical giving listed in 2 Corinthians 8:1–8 provides a set of standards for how dedicated, selfless believers today should give.

GIVING MOTIVATED BY GOD'S GRACE

The first characteristic of biblical giving is that it is motivated by the grace of God. That was the bedrock foundation from which the Macedonians operated: "Now brethren we wish to make known to you the grace of God, which has been given in the churches of Macedonia" (2 Cor. 8:1).

The Macedonians' primary motive for generosity was not human kindness or any other man-centered desire to perform good works. Something extraordinarily beyond what one typically finds in the human heart induced the Macedonians' generous giving. Fallen man's nobility of heart—existing due to his creation in the image of God—allows him to do some things that are humanly good. But even the best of such works cannot and do not reach the proportions of goodness and righteousness that result when acts are motivated by God's grace. That is as true concerning giving as it is with any other activity.

You can witness the inferiority of humanly motivated giving whenever you tune into televised fundraising campaigns, whether secular or religious. Out of the hundreds of pledges phoned, faxed, or e-mailed in, a wealthy individual will occasionally pledge several thousands or tens of thousands to the particular cause. Even though they may be able to afford this type of discretionary spending, they generally stop far short of sacrificial giving. Sometimes you do hear of men and women sacrificing for a noble cause, usually because of some profound and deeply held family attachment. But that's the exception, and human giving generally does not reach the level of sacrifice that alters the giver's lifestyle.

The grace of God is the primary stimulus to biblical giving. A heartfelt longing and earnest desire to give generously and sacrificially flows out of a transformed heart. And along with this transformation, several righteous traits appear within the regenerate person:

- The desire to seek God's kingdom before anything else
- Affections that are fixed in heaven, not on earth
- Love that is centered on God, not the world
- A disposition that hungers and thirsts after righteousness and godliness
- A desire to obey God's Word and follow the Holy Spirit's leading

Giving is simply another effect of transforming grace and appears through the sanctification process. "Work out your salvation with fear and trembling; for it is God who is at work in you, both to will and to work for His good pleasure" (Phil. 2:12–13). Whenever you see someone exhibiting the kind of sacrificial generosity the Macedonian churches had, you know God's grace is at work in that person's heart. They are giving in a biblical manner, way beyond how the unsaved rich or the selfish professed believers give, because they have received the transforming grace of God.

GIVING IN DIFFICULT CIRCUMSTANCES

True biblical giving will also transcend the most difficult of circumstances, which is the second characteristic of biblical giving. Such circumstances had no negative impact on the Macedonians' giving. "That in a great ordeal of affliction their abundance of joy and their deep poverty overflowed in the wealth of their liberality" (2 Cor. 8:2).

The believers in Macedonia easily could have excused themselves from any giving by making one or more statements like: "Well, we can't give right now because we're in extremely difficult times and we don't know what our economic future holds." "We'd better hang on to what little we have because we're being persecuted mercilessly and we don't know if we'll have enough for tomorrow." "We don't think we can get involved in any offering at this time because we have to deal with a lot of hostility from the Jews since we identified with Christ."

Acts 17:1–15 records that the Macedonians really were in some very difficult situations, and Paul's letters corroborate the reality of suffering, affliction, persecution, and tribulation for those churches (Phil. 1:29; 1 Thess. 1:6; 2:14–15; 3:3–10; 2 Thess. 1:4). Yet in the face of those overwhelming, relentless hardships, the Macedonians displayed no "poor me" mentality. They offered no excuses. Instead they gave, even though they were enduring intense, prolonged suffering, and deprivation. That's the way devout Christians react. By God's grace we can always find a way to give, because even the worst circumstances should never hinder our devotion to Jesus Christ and our desire to obey His commands on giving.

GIVING WITH JOY

Third, giving is not righteous unless it's accompanied by sincere, heartfelt joy. That's because joy will supersede any motivation that causes you to give merely out of duty, pressure, fear of punishment if you don't, or simply for the sake of a reward. All of us, at one time or another, have been motivated to give in one of those ways. But we ought to follow the Macedonian example, they looked beyond such mundane factors and gave out of "their abundance of joy" (2 Cor. 8:2).

The Macedonian churches were not just content to be willing givers; they were abundantly happy to give to the Lord. They were already adhering to the apostle Paul's admonition, "So let each one give as he purposes in his heart, not grudgingly or of necessity; for God loves a cheerful giver" (2 Cor. 9:7; NKJV).

Commentator R. C. H. Lenski, describing how the Macedonians gave, said, "They made a joy of robbing themselves." Their devotion to God's kingdom, His local church, and to fellow believers they had never met was profound. Their joy rose above the pain, sorrow, and struggle of difficult circumstances as, for the sake of others, they were happy to divest themselves of what little they had.

The Macedonians had the attitude toward giving that God wants you to have—an unhindered joy that remembers the blessing of laying up treasure in heaven, of giving rather than receiving, and of knowing that God gives back to you in greater measure than what you give to Him.

GIVING WITH GENEROSITY

A fourth characteristic of biblical giving, as exemplified by the Macedonian believers, is unbounded generosity.

Humanly speaking, the Macedonians faced insurmountable difficulties that should have discouraged them from even thinking about giving. Yet Paul says their giving "overflowed in the wealth of their liberality" (2 Cor. 8:2).

That indicates two important aspects of the Macedonians' generosity. First, it was not based on money or possessions. As we have already seen, the churches in Macedonia were not rich materially. But their hearts were rich in an attitude of "liberality," a word that is simply a synonym for generosity. Second, their generosity stemmed from an attitude of single-mindedness. The Greek word rendered "liberality" literally means the opposite of duplicity or double-mindedness. In Scripture it is also translated "sincerity," but more precisely the term conveys the idea of being single-minded. I believe this definition is a wonderful way of seeing what generosity really entails—it is the attitude that triumphs over duplicity.

If you're double-minded about giving, then you're worried too much about your own needs. At best, you're vacillating between concern for yourself and for the needs of others. You might give a small portion, but you'll also hold something back, just in case it's needed.

That was not the attitude of the Macedonian believers. They were rich to overflowing with single-mindedness. That is the attitude God wants you to display when you give. It will help you to stop focusing on yourself and cause you to be more concerned about others (Phil. 2:3–4). You may not be rich in money or possessions, but with the Spirit's help you can be rich in single-minded, selfless, humble devotion to God and the needs of others. As long as you have a generous heart as the Macedonians did, you'll respond with godly generosity whenever there's an opportunity to give.

GIVING WITH PROPORTIONATE SACRIFICE

Fifth, the Macedonians' giving habits are further exemplified by a generosity that was both proportionate and sacrificial. "According to their ability, and beyond their ability, they gave of their own accord" (2 Cor. 8:3).

The Macedonians' individual capability was the starting point for the amount they gave. And that should be your starting point, too, as the apostle Paul elaborates in verse 12, "For if the readiness [to give] is present, it is acceptable according to what a person has, not according to what he does not have." God does not expect you to give what you do not have. All He asks is that you give proportionately, according to your ability. This excludes any concept that says our giving must derive from some fixed percentage or uniform amount. Thus it's reasonable to conclude that the Macedonian Christians gave different amounts, because each of their personal financial situations were different. And that's how it will be with you if you apply the biblical principle of proportionality to your giving.

As the Macedonians gave according to their ability, they also made sure they were doing so in proportions that were sacrificial. Given their impoverished situation and the other difficulties that challenged them, their giving was far beyond what one could ordinarily expect. But those extraordinary believers gladly impoverished themselves even further because of their unwavering faith that God would supply all their needs (Phil. 4:19). With their sacrificial giving they gladly trusted in God for everything so they could help meet the needs of other poor believers in Jerusalem.

The Macedonian churches are a superlative example of people who take Jesus' promises in Matthew 6:25–34 at face value—that if He clothes the lilies and grass of the field, and feeds the birds of the air, He is going to take care of His own. The Macedonians also shared, as we should, David's conviction that sacrificial giving is really the only kind of giving, ". . . I will not offer burnt offerings to the LORD my God which cost me nothing" (2 Sam. 24:24).

GIVING VOLUNTARILY

The sixth characteristic of biblical giving is the twofold truth that it's voluntary and a privilege. Second Corinthians 8:3 concludes by saying, "they gave of their own accord." Literally that means the Macedonians chose their own course of action in their giving. They were self-motivated and spontaneous in giving what they believed the Lord wanted them to give. Neither Paul nor anyone else coerced, manipulated, intimidated, or bribed them into participating in the offering project for the Jerusalem church.

In tandem with the voluntary nature of the Macedonians' giving is the encouraging reality that they viewed the entire ministry of giving as a privilege, not simply an obligation. Paul continues to describe their attitude in 2 Corinthians 8, "Begging us with much urging for the favor of participation in the support of the saints" (v. 4). The Greek vocabulary in this verse reveals just how convinced the believers in Macedonia were that Christian giving is a privilege—such a privilege that they in no way wanted to be left out.

First, they were "begging," a word that is always used in the New Testament to denote a very strong pleading. Second, they were asking for the privilege of giving "with much urging," which means they were making their case aggressively, with a lot of exhortation and importunity. Literally, Paul's original wording says the Macedonians were "coming alongside earnestly, begging for the opportunity" to give.

And last, they were entreating Paul "for the favor of participation in the support of the saints." The phrase "favor of participation" contains two familiar Greek words: *charis,* "favor" or "grace," and *koinonia,* "participation" or "fellowship." The churches of Macedonia were begging for the grace of having a fellowship or partnership in the support of other believers.

Undoubtedly, the Macedonians viewed their giving as a great privilege rather than a mundane obligation. The question is, *How often do you see it that way?* The Macedonians viewed it as a privilege because they knew of no other way for believers to approach the ministry of giving. They were devout Christians, and for them that meant giving was a privilege.

Your attitude will be right in step with the Macedonians' if you're regularly looking for opportunities to give, if you're eager to give, and if you see giving as a blessed privilege that is sometimes worth begging for. That's the kind of outlook that is an integral part of biblical giving.

GIVING WITH WORSHIP AND SUBMISSION

The seventh example of biblical giving far exceeds normal acts of charitable donation or occasional contribution. When you follow the Macedonians' example, it actually rises to the level of spiritual worship. Such an attitude of total dedication is unusual. Even the apostle Paul was pleasantly surprised with the Macedonians' response, "And this, not as we had expected, but they first gave themselves to the Lord and to us by the will of God" (2 Cor. 8:5).

The apostle was simply hoping for a monetary offering, but the Macedonian churches gave themselves—everything they had—in an act of total dedication. This demonstrated that their first priority was to make all they owned completely available and dispensable to the Lord. Such an attitude, supported by the actual exercise of giving, is really the supreme act of worship. It follows the grand pattern set out by Paul in Romans 12:1–2,

> Therefore I urge you, brethren, by the mercies of God, to present your bodies a living and holy sacrifice, acceptable to God, which is your spiritual service of worship. And do not be conformed to this world, but be transformed by the renewing of your mind, so that you may prove what the will of God is, that which is good and acceptable and perfect.

When we praise God and honor His name we are worshiping Him, but the Lord is most pleased when we worship Him by unreservedly offering ourselves. That's the beginning of genuine worship. Once you've unselfishly yielded up to God everything you are, you've begun the life-long process of conducting your "spiritual service of worship," and the giving of everything you have will follow. And that will include being totally free from the materialistic world that enslaves people's thinking and keeps them from giving as they ought. All that happens only as you allow the Spirit to renew your mind, and as you become obedient to God in every area of life, including giving (cf. again Rom. 12:2).

The Macedonian believers were examples of those whose giving was worship. They knew they were "living stones . . . being built up as a spiritual house for a holy priesthood, to offer up spiritual sacrifices acceptable to God through Jesus Christ" (1 Pet. 2:5). That's the way God expects it to be with you and me as well. We are simply stewards who generously and sacrificially offer our resources back to Him.

If biblical giving is worship, it will also be an act of true submission to one's spiritual leaders. The Macedonians' devotion to God led them to submit easily and eagerly to the leadership of their pastors, whether it was to Paul, Timothy, or Titus. They realized that those men were undershepherds of Christ who stood in His place giving direction and leadership to the church in all matters—including giving—and they responded to that godly leadership (cf. 1 Thess. 5:12–13; Heb. 13:17; 1 Pet. 5:5).

Such a submissive response in giving is a challenging example, first to the church at Corinth and now to us, as 2 Corinthians 8:6 suggests, "So we urged Titus that as he had previously made a beginning, so he would also complete in you this gracious work as well." The Macedonians' example prompted Paul, through Titus, to encourage the Corinthians to finally follow through with their year-old pledge to help in the special collection. And it should prompt you to diligent, submissive obedience to your pastors as they lead you to greater faithfulness in the "gracious work" of giving.

GIVING IN LOVE

And lastly, biblical giving is not done in a vacuum or in isolation from other Christian virtues. The Macedonians' exemplary giving flowed out of the complete transformation God's Spirit had wrought in their lives. For your giving to be biblical, it should occur in perfect harmony with all the other positive traits of your regenerate nature, "But just as you abound in everything, in faith and utterance and knowledge and in all earnestness and in the love we inspired in you, see that you abound in this gracious work also" (2 Cor. 8:7).

If your giving is operating right along with other Christian virtues, you're motivated by the greatest virtue of all, love (cf. 1 Cor. 13:3; 1 Pet. 1:22; 1 John 3:17–18). More than anything else, it underscores that your giving is biblical.

You can give without loving (that's merely legalistic, required giving), but you can't love without giving (true affection leads to generosity).

Biblical giving is perhaps the surest way to demonstrate genuine love for others. Paul asks us again to measure ourselves against the example of the Macedonians to verify the quality of our own love, "but as proving through the earnestness of others [the Macedonians] the sincerity of your love also" (2 Cor. 8:8). The true test of sincere love is not positive emotions and good intentions, but tangible actions (James 2:14–18), such as the kind of biblical giving we have described throughout this chapter. Such giving proves that you love the Lord, His church, and those in need. It is the path to God's abundant blessing, a path I trust you're eager to walk.

"He who sows bountifully will also reap bounti-fully."

—2 Corinthians 9:6

Tithing or Voluntary Giving?

I READ AN INTERESTING NEWSPAPER COLUMN recently. It initially caught my eye simply because its headline contained the word *tithe*. When I saw the headline I immediately wondered if the column would deal with the subject scripturally. As I began reading the article I could tell that the writer (Henry Brinton, also a pastor) was not approaching the topic of tithing and church giving from a strictly evangelical perspective, as I would, but nevertheless he provided food for thought, as some of the points in the following excerpt indicate:

> Church services must be free and available to anyone with a spiritual need; but someone has to pay for the upkeep of the church buildings, mission efforts, and salaries. At our church, like most others, the annual budget depends almost entirely on contributions from the membership. The national average is that 20 percent of the people do most of the giving.
>
> Unfortunately, several trends threaten to undermine this pledge base. First, more and more people are coming to church seeking an introduction to God or Jesus, not to learn about the obligations of being part of the congregation.

Research shows that today's younger adults are often believers but not belongers—they have a commitment to their faith, but not necessarily to a congregation.

Now I'm not the kind of pastor who uses high-pressure tactics or only talks about money—honest, you can check my sermon file—but I do confess these trends worry me. One solution might be to send bills to active members with a specific recommendation of what each person should give. "Almost every synagogue sets dues and bills its members," Rabbi Jack Moline of Agudas Achim Congregation in Alexandria, Va., tells me. "Since we do not handle money on Shabbat, when most people gather, we cannot 'pass the plate.' Dues also distribute equitably the burdens of the upkeep of the congregation, rather than depending on those to whom the pastor or fund-raiser has immediate access. At the same time, every synagogue delivers the message with every bill or solicitation that no one will be turned away for lack of resources." While I admire this clear-eyed view of the needs of a Jewish congregation and the responsibility of each member, I doubt it would work in a Protestant church with a long tradition of an offering being a truly free gift.[1]

Mr. Brinton's article reflects much of the uncertainty and misunderstanding, mixed with a few elements of truth, which is prevalent today in religious circles regarding the freedoms and responsibilities of giving. Even in conservative, Bible-believing church contexts people for decades have posed this idea: "Well, I always thought we were supposed to give 10 percent." They're referring to tithing, a term derived from an Old English word that meant to pay or give a tenth part of one's income (both the Hebrew and Greek equivalents are mathematical words meaning "a tenth"). Many Christians through the years have supported tithing, reasoning that because Old Testament patriarchs like Abraham and Jacob gave tithes at certain times, the concept must be God's abiding standard for us. However, the real question they should ask is, "Does the Bible teach tithing as the essential and enduring requirement for Christian giving?" A careful survey of some key texts will give us a clear answer.

THE BASIC ARGUMENT FOR TITHING

In general terms, the typical argument for the practice of tithing goes back to the Old Testament. The Mosaic Law required the Israelites to pay various tithes. Even before the Law, Abraham and Jacob gave tithes to the Lord. Since the practice of tithing appeared before the Law, it must transcend the Law. And that transcendent quality means tithing has to apply after the time of the Law, right down to our day as a universal standard and unchanging requirement.

That argument is seriously flawed for several reasons. First, simply arguing that whatever existed before the Law must exist after the Law poses some real problems. For example, from the Mosaic Law onward, the Jews observed the seventh day of the week as holy unto the Lord and a day of rest. That was the Sabbath law defined in Exodus 20:9–11. But the New Testament, beginning with Jesus' teaching (Mark 2:23–28), clearly sets aside any required Sabbath observance.

Therefore no one is to act as your judge in regard to food or drink or in respect to a festival or a new moon or a Sabbath day—things which are a mere shadow of what is to come; but the substance belongs to Christ (Col. 2:16–17).

One person regards one day above another, another regards every day alike. Each person must be fully convinced in his own mind (Rom. 14:5).

When you consider the existence of the sacrificial system, another problem arises. The offering of animal sacrifices took place as early as Abel's time (Gen. 4:4). A more official, detailed system was established in the Mosaic Law and existed for the remainder of the Old Covenant. But in the New Covenant the ritual of animal sacrifices does not continue—it was superseded by Christ's work on the cross (cf. Heb. 9:11–15; 10:1–14). Today you and I obviously don't offer animals to the Lord. Therefore, just because a certain requirement or practice existed before and during the time of the Law does not make it permanently applicable in the New Covenant.

The argument for tithing, based on Old Testament practices, is even more seriously flawed because tithing both before and after the Law involved two separate issues. You cannot attach one general label to every act of giving. By looking carefully at the Old Testament, you'll see that tithing actually had elements of voluntary and required giving before Moses' time, as it did during and after the Law of Moses. Once you understand that essential distinction—which still operates today—I trust you'll see clearly that no divinely prescribed percentage amount for giving exists now. To reason otherwise reveals a basic misunderstanding of the Old Testament's history and teaching.

GIVING IN THE PRE-MOSAIC ERA

Before we even consider any of the early examples of Old Testament giving, it's important to know that in the Book of Genesis the Hebrew word translated "tithe" did not refer to a required offering, a divine commandment, or an ordinance. Instead, the term refers to a voluntary offering.

Furthermore, the concept of the tithe was not distinctive to the Bible or those who believe in the true God. Historically, the idea of giving a tenth to a deity was a common pagan custom. For nearly all ancient cultures, the number ten was the symbol of completeness. Typically when pagan worshipers wanted to give an offering to their deity they would give a tenth because that symbolized their giving of everything, their surrendering of all they had to the god. So a tenth was a common proportion in many kinds of sacred offerings, and such giving was practiced long before the days of the Hebrew patriarchs. Thus one cannot really argue that God in the Book of Genesis originated and specially mandated tithing as a permanent principle. The concept of tithing is simply not there, as a survey of relevant passages will demonstrate.

Giving from Adam to Noah

Genesis 4 records the first instance of mankind's making an offering to God. Adam's sons Cain and Abel gave voluntary offerings that in no way involved set amounts commanded by God.

In Genesis 4 you can easily infer that the Lord at an earlier time had required that offerings be animal sacrifices. That's what made Cain's fruit, vegetable, and grain offering unacceptable. God accepted Abel's animal sacrifice, but it was not because he had brought a certain percentage of his flock at the right time of the year according to some divine mandate. All the narrative says is that the two brothers each decided voluntarily to bring offerings to God. As far as we can determine, these first offerings were not related to a tenth of anything.

Noah made the second recorded offering in the early days of redemptive history (Genesis 8). Once he observed that the worldwide flood had subsided, Noah wanted to leave the ark and offer a sacrifice to God in gratitude for surviving the immense deluge. Genesis 8:20 says, "Then Noah built an altar to the LORD, and took of every clean animal and of every clean bird and offered burnt offerings on the altar." God didn't command Noah to do that. It was a spontaneous, voluntary offering from the heart—there's no reason to assume it was any sort of tithe.

Giving from Abraham to Moses

Genesis 12:7 contains the next major mention of an offering to God. The Lord had recently called Abraham (then known as Abram) to leave his native land and be the leader of a new nation. In verse 7 God reinforces His promise to Abraham, "The LORD appeared to Abram and said, 'To your descendants I will give this land.' So he built an altar there to the LORD who had appeared to him." Abraham freely responded to the wonderful promise of God that he would be the father of a nation and said, "Thank you, God," by giving Him an offering. Again, there's no divine command and no stipulated percentage to be offered. Abraham simply acted out of the joy and gratitude of his heart (cf. Gen. 13:18). The Hebrew word for "tithe" first appears at the end of Genesis 14:17–20:

> Then after his [Abraham's] return from the defeat of Chedorlaomer and the kings who were with him, the king of Sodom went out to meet him at the valley of Shaveh (that is, the King's Valley). And Melchizedek king of Salem brought out bread and wine; now he was priest of God Most High. He blessed him and said, "Blessed be Abram of God Most High, possessor of heaven and earth; and blessed be God Most High, who has delivered your enemies into your hand." He gave him a tenth of all.

God had just given Abraham a great victory in battle and allowed him to take a valuable amount of spoil. On his way back home Abraham encountered that amazing figure Melchizedek, who was both a king and a priest—a priest of God Most High, the same God whom Abraham worshiped. Abraham was so indebted to God for all He had done for him and how He had protected him, and for the opportunity to meet Melchizedek, that he joyfully and gratefully "gave him [Melchizedek] a tenth of all." Abraham expressed his thanks to God through His representative, Melchizedek the priest.

It's noteworthy that verse 20 does not say Abraham gave a tenth of everything he owned. It was not a tithe of his total income or some kind of annual tithe, but simply a tenth of what he had taken in battle. In fact, it's not recorded anywhere else in the Old Testament that Abraham ever again gave a tithe. So Abraham's tithe was a free, voluntary, one-time action, totally motivated by his heart, not by divine command. The important truth to remember is this: Abraham (through Melchizedek) gave God a tenth of the best, a tenth of the pinnacle of the spoils (as the Greek in Hebrews 7:4 indicates) in recognition of his total commitment and gratitude to the Lord. It's unwise to read anything more into the meaning of Abraham's tithe in Genesis 14.

The only other mention of the tithe prior to the Mosaic Law is in Genesis 28:20–22, the story of Jacob's vow. However, the main lesson to draw from that account is not that we should emulate Jacob's giving a tenth, but that we should avoid his spiritual carnality. Verse 22 actually describes Jacob's attempt to bribe God when he says, "This stone, which I have set up as a pillar, will be God's house, and of all that You give me I will surely give a tenth to You." Jacob was merely doing what the pagans in that region did—gave a tenth to his God, but only if He would conform to his prescription. Jacob was attempting to buy God's blessing in the form of clothing, food, and safe passage (vv. 20–21). His motive for giving a tenth was far from sincere.

If the so-called tithes mentioned in Genesis were not mandatory, is there any significant instance of required giving recorded in the pre-Mosaic era? The answer is yes (Genesis 41); however, such giving still does not fit the contemporary layman's traditional definition of the tithe.

Genesis 41 begins with Pharaoh's dream and Joseph's interpretation of it. Joseph, under divine guidance, accurately interpreted the dream as predicting the coming of seven bountiful years to Egypt, followed by seven years of famine. And here's the way Joseph told Pharaoh to respond to that situation: "Let Pharaoh take action to appoint overseers in charge of the land, and let him exact a fifth of the produce of the land of Egypt in the seven years of abundance" (41:34). Those overseers were the equivalent of ancient IRS agents, whose task would be to collect 20 percent of all that was produced each of the seven years and store it for use during the seven years of famine. Like it or not, that collection was an early version of a national income tax—and it was introduced by God to support the nation of Egypt.

In Genesis 47:24, Joseph reiterates that taxation requirement, "At the harvest you shall give a fifth to Pharaoh, and four-fifths shall be your own for seed of the field and for your food and for those of your households and as food for your little ones." That was required giving. Everyone had to participate in it to support the national government. In contrast, voluntary giving in the days before Moses was directed toward God and was done lovingly, generously, and personally. Neither form of giving was a tithe.

GIVING DURING THE TIME OF THE LAW

As we continue our survey of the Old Testament's teaching on giving, you will see that the Mosaic standards were the same as those during pre-Mosaic times. Certain passages spell out the details of required giving, and others cite instances of voluntary giving.

The Required Tithes

Numbers 18:25–30 (cf. Lev. 27:30) explains how the Levites were to use their tithe, the required giving from the Israelites:

> Then the LORD spoke to Moses, saying, "Moreover, you shall speak to the Levites and say to them, 'When you take from the sons of Israel the tithe which I have given you from them for your inheritance, then you shall present an offering from it to the Lord, a tithe of the tithe. Your offering shall be reckoned to you as the grain from the threshing floor or the full produce from the wine vat. So you shall also present an offering to the LORD from your tithes, which you receive from the sons of Israel; and from it you shall give the LORD's offering to Aaron the priest. Out of all your gifts you shall present every offering due to the LORD, from all the best of them, the sacred part from them. You shall say to them, "When you have offered from it the best of it, then the rest shall be reckoned to the Levites as the product of the threshing floor, and as the product of the wine vat."

God chose the Levites to be priests, to operate the temple, and to lead the theocracy of Israel, the nation run by God. The tithe was the 10 percent taxation used to supply the needs of the Levites, because they had no livelihoods and received no territory when Moses divided the land among the twelve tribes. Essentially, the Israelites gave a tithe every year to support those who ran their government.

The first tithe was a mandatory one tenth of the people's produce and animals. If they didn't give this tithe, the Jews were robbing God because it belonged to Him (Mal. 3:8). Deuteronomy 12:10–11, 17–18 refers to a second annual tithe the Israelites had to pay:

> When you cross the Jordan and live in the land which the LORD your God is giving you to inherit, and He gives you rest from all your enemies around you so that you live in security, then it shall come about that the place in which the LORD your God will choose for His name to dwell, there you shall bring all that I command you: your burnt offerings and your sacrifices, your tithes and the contribution of your hand, and all your choice votive offerings which you will vow to the LORD. . . . You are not allowed to eat within your gates the tithe of your grain or new wine or oil, or the firstborn of your herd or flock, or any of your votive offerings which you vow, or your freewill offerings, or the contribution of your hand. But you shall eat them before the LORD your God in the place which the LORD your God will choose, you and your son and daughter, and your male and female servants, and the Levite who is within your gates; and you shall rejoice before the LORD your God in all your undertakings.

God commanded the Israelites to bring all their offerings, sacrifices, and contributions to Jerusalem, the city He would establish for His name to dwell. He was ordaining support for all the national religious festivals—the ceremonial feasts and celebrations such as Passover. The second tithe was for the sake of the Jews' national religious worship, and it also promoted national unity and fellowship.

Deuteronomy 14:28–29 refers to a third tithe, "At the end of every third year you shall bring out all the tithe of your produce in that year, and shall deposit it in your town. . .and the alien, the orphan and the widow who are in your town, shall come and eat and be satisfied, in order that the LORD your God may bless you in all the work of your hand which you do." That averages out to an additional three and one third percent per year of required giving. The third tithe was known as the welfare tithe, or poor tithe, and was used to help the stranger, the fatherless, and the widowed.

The first three tithes mentioned during Moses' time were nothing more than taxes, and should not be confused with voluntary giving (or "tithing") to the Lord. Those tithes amounted to mandatory taxation that was used to fund Israel's divinely instituted human government.

However, that essential tax base of 23 percent was not the total required giving for people under the Mosaic Law. They had some additional requirements, much as we have gasoline taxes, sales taxes, capital gains taxes, and value added taxes. The Jews had a profit-sharing tax, which was spelled out in Leviticus 19:9–10, "Now when you reap the harvest of your land, you shall not reap the very corners of your field, nor shall you gather the gleanings of your harvest. Nor shall you glean your vineyard, nor shall you gather the fallen fruit of your vineyard; you shall leave them for the needy and for the stranger. I am the LORD your God."

When the people harvested their crops, they were not to gather right up to the corners of their fields, and they were not to retrieve the fruit that fell while they were picking grapes. That was so the poor could go through the fields and vineyards and share in the harvest bounty. (That's what Ruth was doing in the fields in the Book of Ruth.) Such requirements in effect constituted a profit-sharing plan to meet some of the needs of the poor.

In addition to the profit-sharing tax was the requirement for sabbath rest of the farm land every seventh year (Exod. 23:10–11). Every seventh year the people had to forfeit an entire year's normal earnings so the soil could rejuvenate itself. Then there was the annual third of a shekel temple tax. It was used to furnish and maintain the temple.

So the Jews were required to provide a Levites' tithe, a festivals tithe, a poor (welfare) tithe, a profit-sharing tax, the every-seventh-year land sabbath, and the temple tax. All of that calculates out to more than 25 percent in annual income tax to the theocratic government of Israel. It was far more than the simple 10 percent many believers mistakenly cite to bolster their argument for required tithing today.

The Voluntary Giving

Voluntary giving under the Mosaic Law was done in addition to the required giving. And just as before Moses, freewill giving was proportionate, generous, sacrificial, and from the heart.

First of all, Numbers 18:12 describes the principle of first fruit, "All the best of the fresh oil and all the best of the fresh wine and of the grain, the first fruits of those which they give to the LORD, I give them to you." God set the example of giving the very best to the Levites of what the people had offered to Him. Therefore, if we want to be pleasing to Him in our giving, we should give the Lord the first and best of what we earn. When you give from the top like this—from the cream of the crop—you're giving God what you have and believing Him for what you don't have.

When people trusted God and were willing to give Him the first fruits, even if they didn't know exactly how much they would have, He abundantly rewarded and blessed them, "Honor the LORD from your wealth and from the first of all your produce; so your barns will be filled with plenty and your vats will overflow with new wine" (Prov. 3:9–10; cf. 11:24). That's the essence of freewill giving. It's a generous amount, given by faith, from the best of our resources.

Second, the Book of Exodus illustrates that God is most concerned with the giver's heart attitude in voluntary giving. There were no posters or banners placed around the camp of Israel with printed reminders such as, "Have you given your tithe yet?" Such contemporary-style motivational devices weren't needed because the people gave whatever amount they desired and purposed in their hearts. The following verses from Exodus demonstrate that truth:

> Moses spoke to all the congregation of the sons of Israel, saying, "This is the thing which the LORD has commanded, saying, 'Take from among you a contribution to the LORD; whoever is of a willing heart, let him bring it as the LORD's contribution: gold, silver, and bronze.'" (Exod. 35:4–5)

> Everyone whose heart stirred him and everyone whose spirit moved him came and brought the LORD's contribution for the work of the tent of meeting and for all its service and for the holy garments. Then all whose hearts moved them, both men and women, came and brought brooches and earrings and signet rings and bracelets, all articles of gold; so did every man who presented an offering of gold to the LORD. (Exod. 35:21–22)

> The Israelites, all the men and women, whose heart moved

them to bring material for all the work, which the LORD had commanded through Moses to be done, brought a freewill offering to the LORD. (Exod. 35:29)

And they said to Moses, "The people are bringing much more than enough for the construction work which the LORD commanded us to perform." So Moses issued a command, and a proclamation was circulated throughout the camp, saying, "Let no man or woman any longer perform work for the contributions of the sanctuary." Thus the people were restrained from bringing any more. (Exod. 36:5–6)

Today seldom do you see churches so consistently giving as generously and proportionately as the Israelites did (cf. Deut. 16:10, 17; 1 Chron. 29:9–10, 16). That's freewill giving from the heart—and as with the giving for the tabernacle, it will sometimes even greatly exceed the present needs—and is according to the Lord's design and will.

GIVING IN NEW TESTAMENT TIMES

The next logical question to ask in our brief survey of what the Scripture says about "tithing" is, "Does the New Testament teach the same giving pattern as we've just seen in the Old Testament?" The answer is an unqualified yes. In fact, the New Testament contains an exact parallel to the Old Testament's teaching—there are still two kinds of giving: required and voluntary.

Required giving in Jesus' time still existed in the form of the Mosaic taxation system. Many of the elements of the theocracy were still operative. The Levites, Pharisees, and Sadducees possessed all the real political power and ran the government, under the direction of the occupying Romans.

The wall of the temple courtyard had trumpet-shaped receptacles into which the people dropped their tax money. They were careful to do that as their duty and responsibility to the religious leaders.

In addition, the Gospels refer to the exorbitant tax burden the Romans, through Jewish collectors (publicans), imposed on the people (cf. Matt. 5:46–47; Mark 2:14–16; Luke 5:29–30; 19:2, 8). In spite of that extra taxation, which was generally unfair and universally hated by the Jews, Jesus never commented on the equity of it. Instead, He upheld the Old Testament principle and taught that we should pay our taxes. Matthew's Gospel records Jesus' basic teaching on taxes this way:

> When they came to Capernaum, those who collected the two-drachma tax [temple tax] came to Peter and said, "Does your teacher not pay the two-drachma tax?" He said, "Yes." And when he came into the house, Jesus spoke to him first, saying, "What do you think, Simon? From whom do the kings of the earth collect customs or poll-tax, from their sons or from strangers?" When Peter said, "From strangers," Jesus said to him, "Then the sons are exempt. However, so that we do not offend them, go to the sea and throw in a hook, and take the first fish that comes up; and when you open its mouth, you will find a shekel. Take that and give it to them for you and Me." (Matt. 17:24–27)

On the one hand, Jesus was saying that, as the Son of the Father, He did not have to pay any taxes, and neither did His followers, who are children of their heavenly Father. But, lest he or his Master offend those in authority, Jesus told Peter to pay the temple tax. Our Lord's words are also a good reminder that we should pay our taxes because God is behind all human government and He ordained whatever tax system we're under (Rom. 13:1–7; 1 Pet. 2:13; cf. Matt. 22:15–22).

There are just two mentions of the actual word *tithe* in the Gospels, and both instances refer to taxation, or required giving. In Matthew 23:23, Jesus told the Pharisees, "Woe to you, scribes and Pharisees, hypocrites! For you tithe mint and dill and cummin, and have neglected the weightier provisions of the law: justice and mercy and faithfulness; but these are the things you should have done without neglecting the others." Jesus' sharp criticism of the religious leaders did not concern the tithe. He simply acknowledged that they paid it as part of the Mosaic requirements. In a sense, Christ commended them for not neglecting their duty. Here His main concern was that the Pharisees had hypocritically ignored the higher moral principles of the Law.

Similarly, Luke 18:12 in the parable of the Pharisee and the tax collector (18:9–14) refers to the paying of tithes. The Pharisee was actually boasting about paying his taxes, and that attitude made no sense because we are supposed to pay taxes anyway. Jesus did not commend or condemn the concept of tithing, because that was not His point in this parable. His purpose was to illustrate the fallacy of trusting in one's own righteousness for justification.

Hebrews 7:4–9 contains several references to tenths and tithes, but again not as directives or instructions for contemporary church practice. The passage is simply a recollection of the historical event of Abraham meeting Melchizedek, an Old Testament event we discussed earlier in this chapter. The writer's point concerns the priesthood of Christ, who is a priest after the order of Melchizedek.

Therefore, among all the New Testament references to a tithe or 10 percent, there is no command to believers about the necessity of 10 percent. That's because tithing has never been an offering to God—it was always a form of taxation to support the government.

The Bible's teaching about tithing versus voluntary giving is clear. Tithing in both Old and New Testament times was the paying of taxes, and the Jews under the Mosaic Law paid as much as 25 percent per year in tithes (that's far more than 10 percent). For years, many conservative, evangelical, and fundamentalist churches—denominational and nondenominational—have promoted tithing as the basic standard for what their members should place in the offering plate. But such a rigid concept, viewed as a universal and eternal principle for all believers, simply is not taught in Scripture.

The New Covenant principle on giving—the one you and I should live by—is not derived from some mandatory percentage. New Covenant giving flows from the heart and is personally determined; it is based on the model and exhibits the characteristics we discussed in chapters 5 and 6 of this book. Second Corinthians 9:6–7 is an excellent summary of how we should give to the Lord, "He who sows bountifully will also reap bountifully. Each one must do just as he has purposed in his heart, not grudgingly or under compulsion, for God loves a cheerful giver."

8

"(Giving) is acceptable according to what a person has, not according to what he does not have."

—2 Corinthians 8:12

8 Stewardship with Integrity

WHAT IS STEWARDSHIP? It is somewhat of an old-fashioned term that dates its origin back to the fifteenth century, but its modern dictionary definition, "the individual's responsibility to manage his life and property with proper regard to the rights of others," suggests a practical relevance to our study of giving. With many pastors, elders, and deacons in local churches, *stewardship* is virtually synonymous with the giving program. And I believe that is a valid association. Stewardship encompasses the whole idea of giving to spiritual causes and funding kingdom enterprises—investing in eternity by means of the church, so that the body of Christ might carry out its ministry, which sometimes includes meeting the physical and financial needs of its own people.

Of course, such a definition of stewardship must be concerned with the matter of integrity. That's because so many people feel strongly that any instruction and admonition about money and giving in the church is unacceptable, intrusive, and even offensive. They often criticize the church for being preoccupied with fundraising, and sometimes their criticism is valid because many conmen, hucksters, and charlatans have appeared throughout church history. Those fraudulent leaders have used various schemes to enrich themselves and advance their own causes, all at the expense of unsuspecting church members and in the place of scriptural purposes that honor God and advance His kingdom.

Legitimate, honest, and biblical church leaders must be sensitive to those concerns about abuse and vigilant in opposing them. However, when we have finished condemning all the ungodly and unscriptural stewardship practices, that does not change the truth that giving is a central, God-ordained element in the life of the church. There is nothing wrong with a church's placing a high priority on the weekly collection. Members' giving, as a part of their worship, is the means for advancing God's kingdom, glorifying His name, and assisting people truly in need. However, as with anything else in the church, a stewardship program must be conducted with the utmost integrity.

Second Corinthians 8:10—9:5 is one of the most personal, practical, and straightforward sections of Scripture. It is the prime passage from which to glean the apostle Paul's indispensable principles of a stewardship program with integrity. As we've seen earlier in our study of giving, 2 Corinthians 8—9 pertains to Paul's project of collecting money from the Gentile churches to aid the impoverished Jerusalem church. You can use this particular passage (8:10—9:5) as a measuring stick by which to judge all future monetary appeals that may come your way. Whether it is your church's stewardship program or the fundraising campaign of a parachurch ministry, the plan should contain Paul's principles of integrity in giving.

THE GIVING WILL BE VOLUNTARY

The first essential element of integrity that any credible stewardship program will have is the now-familiar concept of voluntary giving. Second Corinthians 8:10 says, "I give my opinion in this matter, for this is to your advantage, who were the first to begin a year ago not only to do this, but also to desire to do it." Paul assumes the Corinthians already know giving is important and commanded by God. But as far as an amount, the apostle is not issuing a command. As we have already seen, the amount any believer gives is up to the individual, based on his or her heart attitude before the Lord. The ultimate issue for the Corinthians, or for you and me, is how much advantage we would like as a result of our giving. How much do we want the Lord to bless us? (Luke 6:38; Acts 20:35; 2 Cor. 9:6; cf. Luke 16:9–12)

It is so crucial for any stewardship campaign to have the element of voluntarism because many of us remember the terrible harm that can occur when that principle is ignored. Two notorious incidents just in the past twenty-five years illustrate what I mean. First was the Jonestown tragedy in northern South America in 1978, and then the sad episode of the Branch Davidians in 1993 in Texas. Both cases involved extreme demagogic leadership (Jim Jones and David Koresh, respectively) persuading and misleading people in the name of a false brand of Christianity. In both situations, people relinquished all their money and possessions, and agreed to an arrangement in which all the wealth was used at the discretion of one "spokesman for God." That kind of forced giving, which really amounts to a confiscation and reallocation of resources, never characterizes stewardship with integrity.

Unquestionably, the first standard by which to measure the integrity of any stewardship program is: Are the people encouraged to support it voluntarily, out of their own heartfelt desire to receive God's blessing? If you are intimidated to participate, presented with mandatory amounts or percentages to contribute, or in any way manipulated, the stewardship appeal is not scriptural.

THE GIVING WILL BE COMPLETED

The second principle of stewardship with integrity calls for faithfulness to complete the project, as Paul told the Corinthians, "But now finish doing it also, so that just as there was the readiness to desire it, so there may be also the completion of it by your ability" (2 Cor. 8:11). Those who are the recipients of stewardship appeals must also demonstrate integrity by actually giving their intended contribution. Initial good intentions are almost meaningless if you don't follow through and help complete a particular project (cf. Luke 9:62).

One of the hardest church leadership burdens to bear is dealing with good beginnings that aren't finished. At the church in Corinth, the members' resolve to complete their giving was likely dampened by certain false teachers' attacks on Paul's personal integrity. Those teachers accused him of being untrustworthy and deceitful, that he was in the ministry only for the money. But since Titus had told them the truth about Paul's intentions and Paul himself had defended his overall integrity (2 Cor. 6:1–10; 7:5–7, 13–16), it was time for the Corinthians to finish their commitment to the offering.

It's difficult for most Christians to maintain resolve and complete something important like a stewardship project. So many distractions, interruptions, and side issues—not to mention natural apathy—can get in the way and prevent us from finishing well. As with everything else in the Christian walk, keeping a biblical focus in our stewardship is a matter of discipline, dedication, and staying focused on the truth. The point is simply this: if by godly discernment and scriptural guidance you at one time believed that a stewardship plan was God's will for you, that divine purpose likely has not changed and you ought to demonstrate faithfulness in completing your personal commitment. This certainly includes keeping any promise you make to give.

THE GIVING WILL BE PROPORTIONATE

If a stewardship program has genuine integrity, it will ask for contributions that are in proportion to what people have. That element is simply a characteristic of any biblical giving, as we discussed in chapter 6 of this book (cf. also 1 Cor. 16:2; 2 Cor. 8:3).

The apostle Paul strengthens the emphasis on proportionality with his final three words in 2 Corinthians 8:11, "by your ability." And then he further underscores his point with this instruction: "For if the readiness is present, it is acceptable according to what a person has, not according to what he does not have" (v. 12).

Those who use integrity in raising funds will not ask people to give more than they have, to go into debt, or to pledge some minimum amount or percentage. They will instead adhere to what the Word teaches and remind believers that God is asking them to give out of whatever resource they have, not according to some impossible standard they can't meet.

All God is really after, and a sound stewardship program will reiterate this, is the heart attitude in our giving. In certain circumstances, God's Spirit may lovingly prompt you to stretch to the limits of your ability (or beyond your normal giving level), and you may choose to adjust your budget to meet that special stricture. But the Lord does not place such demands on every believer legalistically and uniformly. Simply put, He never asks us to give more than our present resources permit, just proportionately, according to what we have.

THE GIVING WILL BALANCE THE RESOURCES IN THE BODY OF CHRIST

Another very significant but often-misunderstood element of any biblical stewardship plan is that the giving will balance the resources in the body of Christ. Paul asserts the importance of this in his instructions to the Corinthian believers:

> For this is not for the ease of others and for your affliction, but by way of equality—at this present time your abundance being a supply for their need, so that their abundance also may become a supply for your need, that there may be equality; as it is written, "He who gathered much did not have too much, and he who gathered little had no lack." (2 Cor. 8:13–15)

What is Paul saying here? Basically, he's anticipating the potential criticism of his opponents in Corinth that, as a Jew, he was partial toward the Jerusalem church. According to his critics, Paul's offering project was merely a way to make amends to the Jewish believers for his early persecution of them (cf. Acts 8:1–3; 9:1–2). In essence, Paul's opponents would likely argue that he was asking Gentile believers to make huge sacrifices of their resources, so Paul's friends in Jerusalem could be more comfortable and not have to sacrifice.

Paul anticipates that criticism by saying he was not calling for the comparatively rich Gentiles to become poor so the impoverished Jewish believers could become rich. The real issue, according to Paul, is one of "equality" in the church. The Greek word rendered "equality" in verse 13 could better be translated "balance" or "equilibrium." It is *isotatos,* from which we derive the scientific term *isostasy,* the study of the earth's balance. Just as isostasy helps us understand that God designed the earth with high mountains and deep seas that compensate for each other and keep the earth rotating in perfect balance, Paul's use of *isotatos* indicates that God desires a certain kind of balance within His church.

From time to time, situations will arise in which a group of believers with more can help other believers with less. Paul is saying that if you're in the group with resources it is your spiritual responsibility as a member of the body of Christ to lovingly help those in the other group—to bring some balance or equality among the parts of His body.

However, that concept of equality within the church must be clearly understood. Paul was not using "equality" the way contemporary advocates of homosexual rights, women's rights, or animal rights do. And the expression does not refer to some form of socialist, Marxist economic egalitarianism. Therefore, Paul's words should not be confused with any sort of plan to redistribute funds in the misguided fashion of the modern welfare state, with all its abuses.

Of course one of those abuses is the tendency for welfare recipients to become indolent. But Paul addressed that issue in 2 Thessalonians 3:10, "For even when we were with you, we used to give you this order: if anyone is not willing to work, then he is not to eat, either."

So the issue for a stewardship program that creates balance within the body of Christ is not that it would produce a class of idle takers who are made lazy and comfortable at the expense of the givers. Stewardship with integrity simply tries to help people who have already done all they can to meet their own basic needs but can't because of extenuating circumstances. It realizes that believers are not isolated and independent people, but members of the family of God and responsible to meet the needs of each other in love.

In 2 Corinthians 8:15 Paul further illustrates the principle of balance among believers by quoting part of a verse from the Exodus 16:13–18 narrative. That passage introduces the story of manna from heaven and tells in part what the Israelites learned about God's balanced provision:

> In the morning there was a layer of dew around the camp. When the layer of dew evaporated, behold, on the surface of the wilderness there was a fine flake-like thing, fine as the frost on the ground. When the sons of Israel saw it, they said to one another, "What is it?" For they did not know what it was. And Moses said to them, "It is the bread which the LORD has given you to eat. This is what the LORD has commanded, 'Gather of it every man as much as he should eat; you shall take an omer apiece according to the number of persons each of you has in his tent.'" The sons of Israel did so, and some gathered much and some little. When they measured it with an omer, he who had gathered much had no excess, and he who had gathered little had no lack; every man gathered as much as he should eat.

It was just natural that some of the Israelites gathered a lot of manna and others were able to gather only a little. Adults in their prime were able to pick up more than the weaker elderly or the inexperienced children. Also, some were hedging against the future by gathering as much manna as they could at one time, not knowing how much longer God would provide that unique food.

But verse 18 says God made sure the gathering of manna worked out in a balanced way. When it was all measured out, there was enough for everybody. And it went like that day after day. By analogy, that's how God wants the basic needs of His children in the body of Christ met. Some of us have more, some less, but in the end we make sure we meet the basic needs of everyone.

THE GIVING WILL BE DIRECTED BY GODLY LEADERSHIP

Whenever I hear about a financial undertaking or a stewardship campaign somewhere within the body of Christ—a church needs money, a parachurch ministry needs funds, a missionary is seeking to raise support—I always ask the question, Who's behind the effort? It's easy for strong personalities who are powerful communicators, clever motivators, and ingenious entrepreneurs to get thousands of donations to fill their coffers. But the real issue is not how dynamic and successful such men are, but how accountable they are to spiritual oversight and how devoted they are to God. I want to give my money to a ministry that's led by godly pastors and elders who have been gifted and appointed to oversee the church according to biblical principles. I want to make sure the project is overseen by men who love Christ, walk in the Spirit, have a solid grasp of Scripture, and embrace sound theology. Any stewardship program with genuine integrity will meet these important concerns.

Paul knew that to operate a God-honoring stewardship program it had to be more than a one-man show. With his special collection for the Jerusalem church he realized he had to answer the criticism that it was merely his own pet project. He had to disarm those critics at Corinth who claimed his enterprise was not credible because it was not accountable to anyone else. His words do just that.

In 2 Corinthians 8:16–17 we see again how effectively

Paul anticipated potential disapproval: "But thanks be to God who puts the same earnestness on your behalf in the heart of Titus. For he not only accepted our appeal, but being himself very earnest, he has gone to you of his own accord." This is the apostle's great affirmation that his desire to raise money for the Jerusalem church was not just an individual passion. Paul proclaims that Titus, another godly man and faithful, trustworthy servant-leader of the church (cf. 2 Cor. 7:13–15), was in wholehearted agreement with the plan.

Titus's support of Paul's stewardship plan strengthened the entire enterprise and dispelled needless doubts in the minds of potential supporters such as the Corinthians. The Lord, in using the gentile Titus, showed the Corinthian Church that Paul was not operating under compulsion, and his plan was something far broader than a personal "Jewish" project to benefit the Jerusalem church. Paul could have unilaterally pushed ahead with his collection project, the way so many contemporary fundraising mobilizers do. But he sought unanimity of heart and purpose, and God granted that to him in the person of Titus. It is so encouraging when godly men all affirm a stewardship project and together move forward with it. When that happens, you can be assured it exemplifies stewardship with integrity and is according to the will and purpose of God.

Stewardship under the direction of godly and doctrinally sound pastors will also exhibit a careful accountability. Paul knew he could trust himself and Titus in anything pertaining to the special collection. But his enemies potentially could bring reproach on his efforts by stirring up the seeds of dissension and accusation that lingered around the church at Corinth. He didn't want them to have even the slightest opportunity to seize upon some minor mishandling of the money and thereby discredit the gospel.

With those potential problems in mind, Paul provided additional accountability for what he was doing when he said, "We have sent along with him [Titus] the brother whose fame in the things of the gospel has spread through all the churches; and not only this, but he has also been appointed by the churches to travel with us in this gracious work, which is being administered by us for the glory of the Lord Himself, and to show our readiness" (2 Cor. 8:18–19).

The churches (probably from Macedonia), undoubtedly with Paul's approval, appointed a representative to help administer the collection. He was an unnamed but well-known preacher of unimpeachable character, no doubt respected and loved by all the believers in the region. Unlike so many churches today, the Macedonians, though they planned wisely, did not enlist some savvy fundraiser or schemer to help with important stewardship matters. Instead, those early Christians selected a godly pastor whose humble leadership was proved beyond question. And all those precautions were taken "so that no one will discredit us in our administration of this generous gift; for we have regard for what is honorable, not only in the sight of the Lord, but also in the sight of men" (vv. 20–21).

When ministry becomes challenging and arduous, it's tempting to respond this way: "As long as we act appropriately before God, who cares what people think?" But that does not honor the Lord, especially regarding our stewardship. Paul knew that it mattered what unbelievers think because so many of them, like his enemies at Corinth, are quick to find fault with the church. And one of the areas most targeted has been believers' lack of integrity in financial practices. We must handle money honestly and with accountability so people can see our integrity as a manifestation of our righteousness (cf. Prov. 3:4; Rom. 12:17).

Paul even took an extra step to ensure complete accountability, "We have sent with them [Titus and the preacher] our brother, whom we have often tested and found diligent in many things, but now even more diligent because of his great confidence in you" (2 Cor. 8:22). The Greek ("tested and found diligent") indicates that the third brother was proven (like metals that have passed the test) and zealous for the Lord. The apostle made sure there would be careful accountability and proper administration of all the collection money by having three trustworthy men, well-known for their godly character, carry the funds to Jerusalem.

You can trust that a stewardship effort has integrity and is worthy of your full support if it is directed by and accountable to men like Paul and his associates. When servants who walk most closely with Christ take care of the church's finances, critics trying to undermine the extension of God's kingdom are silenced. And God's people have a right to such biblical accountability.

THE GIVING WILL BE AN EXPRESSION OF LOVE

If the Lord is laying on your heart the support of a particular stewardship appeal and the right precautions for accountability are there, the next step is to freely and lovingly give what God wants you to give. Such an expression of giving is another trademark of stewardship with integrity.

Absolutely nothing is more characteristic of love than generous, lavish giving, as Paul reminded the Corinthians in his further instruction to them about their need to support the Jerusalem collection: "Therefore openly before the churches, show them the proof of your love and of our reason for boasting about you" (2 Cor. 8:24). Our testimony is linked to our love (John 13:34–35), and our love is measured by our generosity. We, the Corinthian believers, or anyone else who claims to follow Christ can say we have love, but until we display it, that love is meaningless (1 John 3:18).

When someone falls in love, he or she is extremely generous toward the one loved. Parents who really love their children can hardly restrain themselves from giving as much as possible to them. When we love a very good friend, we regularly want to give things to them. That's just how love responds. So expressions of love from one believer to another will be integral elements of stewardship with integrity.

THE GIVING WILL SET AN EXAMPLE FOR OTHERS

Stewardship with integrity will also feature giving that sets an excellent example—it provides a high standard for others to strive toward. Such a superior example of generous giving ought to be the goal for every local church. As a pastor, I envision my church or any other local assembly of believers fulfilling this aspect of stewardship in three basic steps.

First, the people should give enough to meet all the church's needs. There should be no shortfall of resources. Whatever basic ministry commitments exist, whatever basic expenses need to be paid, there should be enough money to cover those obligations.

Second, the people should give more than the church needs. They should give so their church can expand its ministries by supporting more missionaries, providing more assistance for those truly in need (through a deacons' fund), having more printed material for local outreach, and training more people within the church.

And third, simply giving more than enough should not be the ultimate goal for a church stewardship program. Ideally, the people should give so generously and magnanimously that their congregation becomes *the* standard by which other believers measure church giving. That was Paul's great hope for the Corinthian church as he moved toward the close of his instructions to them about the special offering:

> For it is superfluous for me to write to you about this ministry to the saints; for I know your readiness, of which I boast about you to the Macedonians, namely, that Achaia has been prepared since last year, and your zeal has stirred up most of them. But I have sent the brethren, in order that our boasting about you may not be made empty in this case, so that, as I was saying, you may be prepared; otherwise if any Macedonians come with me and find you unprepared, we—not to speak of you—will be put to shame by this confidence. (2 Cor. 9:1–4)

In the beginning it was the Corinthians' stewardship example that motivated the Macedonian churches and made them the model we discussed in chapter 6 of this book. The apostle Paul simply wanted the Corinthians to continue being exemplars in the area of giving. He knew that a church that doesn't give or barely meets its own financial needs sets a dishonorable example, whereas a faithful church that gives far beyond just what's needed to meet basic needs can be a role model for all other churches. He was not satisfied with giving that is marginal or second best; and we shouldn't be either, if our churches really wish to display a standard of excellence in giving.

COVETOUSNESS WILL NOT BE AN OBSTACLE

If a stewardship plan in your church meets all the criteria for integrity that we've outlined in this chapter and the Spirit convinces you that it deserves your proportional support, but you don't participate—there is a sin issue you must deal with. You can't honestly say you favor the program if that scenario describes you, because stewardship with integrity involves giving that overcomes the sin of covetousness. Paul identified that truth when he told the Corinthians, "So I thought it necessary to urge the brethren that they would go on ahead to you and arrange beforehand your previously promised bountiful gift, so that the same would be ready as a bountiful gift and not affected by covetousness" (2 Cor. 9:5).

The word translated "covetousness" could also be rendered "greed." It denotes a grasping to acquire more and hold on to it at the expense of others. Such thoughts and behaviors are rooted in selfishness and pride. Few sins are portrayed as more ugly or condemned more clearly in Scripture than the sin of covetousness (Ps. 10:3; Eccles. 5:10; Mic. 2:2–3; Mark 7:21–23; 1 Cor. 6:9–10; Eph. 5:3; 1 Tim. 6:10; 2 Pet. 2:14). In fact, Paul felt so strongly about the evils of covetousness that his admonition to the Corinthian believers, and us, is not even to associate with people who practice it: "But actually I wrote to you not to associate with any so-called brother if he is an immoral person, or covetous, or an idolater. . .not even to eat with such a one" (1 Cor. 5:11).

More than once, Paul equated covetousness with idolatry (Eph. 5:5; Col. 3:5). If you have the opportunity and the resources to give when you know God wants you to participate, and you don't, you are worshiping an idol instead of God. Your idol may be clothes, home furnishings, electronics, recreational gear, a car, a vacation, or whatever else. None of those things is intrinsically bad, but if they hinder or prevent you from worshiping God through generous giving, they are the idols of covetousness.

In the end, the only obstacle to stewardship campaigns

that have integrity is covetousness. It comes down to a battle of your heart and mind. If there's a conviction in your heart to support a legitimate appeal for gifts, do so; don't yield to the temptation of covetousness. Stewardship programs succeed and exhibit godly integrity because Christians give in a manner that proves they have overcome covetousness.

I trust this chapter has helped you understand the crucial role integrity plays in any stewardship program. Today when we are saturated with solicitations and appeals of every conceivable variety and from all quarters, both inside and outside the church, integrity is the barometer we must look to if we want to discern the credibility of a stewardship plan. In addition to the principles from 2 Corinthians 8–9 we've explored, consider the following list of questions in evaluating the integrity of any fundraising effort that claims to be spiritual and worthy of your support.

- Does the ministry have a definite and personal commitment to Christ?
- Does it have an unclouded commitment to the authority of Scripture?
- Is its mission a biblical one with biblical objectives?
- Does its operation reflect a definite eternal perspective?
- Do the ministry's leaders depend prayerfully on God more than on contemporary marketing strategies and fundraising techniques?
- Is there obvious love and concern for those ministered to?
- Is there evidence of spiritual maturity, Christlikeness, and integrity?
- Do the leaders have a spirit of servanthood and humility rather than presumption and arrogance? Does the fundraising enrich them personally?
- Does the ministry present a modest and unpretentious image?

- Has the ministry been accountable with its funds and used them for the stated purposes?
- Are the appeals free of a continual "crisis tone" that says the success or failure of the ministry depends on *your* gift?
- Does the ministry recognize its responsibility and submission to the leadership of the local church?
- Are there scriptural and godly relationships among the ministry staff?
- Does the ministry have a track record of spiritual fruit? Have you seen some evidence of that fruit?

If you can honestly answer yes to all these questions, you can freely, joyfully and generously support such a ministry knowing that it is conducting stewardship that honors God with genuine integrity.

9

The generous Christian never needs to fear not having enough. That's because the more you give, the more God gives in return.

The True Path to Prosperity

THE "PROSPERITY GOSPEL" is still alive and well in some sectors of contemporary Christianity. That's the teaching that says God wants His followers to be rich and have all the best from life—large, elaborate homes, expensive luxury cars, the most ostentatious wardrobes, and so on. That greed-driven heresy is popular because it declares that God's primary function is to dole out material goods to His people. The doctrine most often appears in the modern Charismatic movement under various labels—the Word Faith movement, the Faith Formula, Word of Faith movement, Positive Confession, or Name It and Claim It.[1] This appeals to people by essentially telling about a type of Christianized "voodoo" that can be used to cajole and manipulate God for their own selfish gain whenever they want. The movement claims to be able to teach people (for *lots* of remuneration) how to plug into the right spiritual wavelength so that God will deliver all the money and goods imaginable to please every personal indulgence.

The secular culture also makes false appeals for how to be prosperous by working hard, earning as much money as possible, then hoarding, saving, and investing your money as shrewdly as possible. It claims that is the only way to increase your net worth and guarantee a prosperous retirement.

Neither of those get-rich philosophies, however, can match God's true path to prosperity. The Lord is concerned about your material needs, and He really does have a plan for your financial prosperity that promises to meet your every need. He does not disregard hard work, saving, or wise investing, but He does reject aberrations like the prosperity gospel and man-centered methods based on accumulation and hoarding. God's plan for the believer's genuine prosperity, as outlined in His Word, is simply this: *You and I must give away what we have.*

Second Corinthians 9:6–15, the final section of the apostle Paul's great instruction to the Corinthians on giving, elucidates God's path to prosperity as well as any passage in Scripture. Paul develops his argument on the foundation of well-established Old Testament truth. Proverbs 11:24–25 says, "There is one who scatters, and yet increases all the more, and there is one who withholds what is justly due, and yet results only in want. The generous man will be prosperous, and he who waters will himself be watered" (cf. 19:17; Luke 6:38; Gal. 6:7–9). The generous Christian never needs to fear not having enough. That's because the more you give, the more God gives in return.

THE PRINCIPLE OF SOWING AND REAPING

Paul begins his instruction on God's true path to prosperity with a familiar axiom that utilizes agricultural imagery: "Now this I say, he who sows sparingly will also reap sparingly, and he who sows bountifully will also reap bountifully" (2 Cor. 9:6). Every farmer knows that if you sow a little seed you get a little crop. The greater the amount of crop that begins in seed form, the greater the amount that can appear in the form of grain later. The spiritual analogy is just as straightforward: The more money you sow to help advance God's kingdom, the greater harvest of divine blessing you'll realize. This is the culmination of Paul's effort to motivate the Corinthian church to give generously to the struggling believers in Jerusalem and to motivate all of us to give faithfully to the local church and the work of God around the world.

The Holy Spirit in verse 6 graciously prompts us toward that end by twice using the Greek word translated "bountifully." That is a proper translation of the term in this context, but inherent in the word's meaning is also the concept of blessing. In a sense, the person who sows or gives with the idea of blessing others will in turn receive a blessing. That may seem an extravagant principle, but it isn't. Those who give with the right attitude know that the more they offer to God, the more blessing He is going to return to them in the harvest.

Nevertheless, some who read about this principle of maximum blessing may respond by asking, "Isn't such motivation all wrong, merely appealing to our greed and self-interest?" To that I would answer no and simply remind them that God, through His Word, promises believers all kinds of rewards (e.g., Ps. 16:11; 73:24; Prov. 11:18; Is. 64:4; Matt. 5:12; 19:21; 25:21, 34; John 14:2; Rom. 2:7; 8:18; 1 Cor. 3:11–14; 9:25; Phil. 3:14; Col. 3:24; 2 Tim. 4:8; Heb. 9:15; James 1:12; 2 John 8; Rev. 2:10; 22:12). God's gracious promise to reward us according to the measure of what we sow is simply one of those promises. It is not an appeal to the hypocritical, self-interested person who merely professes faith and pretends to have the right attitude in his or her giving. Instead, it's a tremendous motivation to all pure-hearted believers.

THE BENEFITS OF THE HARVEST

The only important questions that remain as potential hindrances to our fully enjoying the true path to prosperity are these: What is the bounty or the harvest that God promises? Is it spiritual or material? If God's blessing is merely spiritual, what's the point in our giving generously if we can't eat, wear, drive, or spend the dividends? Second Corinthians 9:7–15 completely answers those questions by revealing five benefits of God's harvest, both material and spiritual, that flow out from one another and culminate in the greatest practical blessings you or I could ever imagine.

Love from God

The apostle Paul writes of the first harvest benefit in 2 Corinthians 9:7, "Each one must do just as he has purposed in his heart, not grudgingly or under compulsion, for God loves a cheerful giver." The first benefit you realize when you give generously, then, is *love from God*. This is a unique promise in Scripture, the only place where God grants a special display of His love to believers because of their particular behavior. We know God loves the world in a certain way (John 3:16), and He loves His own in a more wonderful way (John 10:27–30; 13:1). But even among the elect, there are some for whom He has an even more special affection—the cheerful givers.

Every Christian can experience this intense and special love from God (it's from *agapao* in the Greek, the strongest term for love). All we have to do is give to the Lord "just as he has purposed in his heart, not grudgingly or under compulsion." Again, the elements of personal, voluntary, and proportionate giving are present, but not in some casual fashion. "Has purposed" in the original means to act from a predetermination rather than from an impulse. We should carefully think about and predetermine what we will give and then do whatever our heart has told us to do.

God says there is only one way to give, and that's cheerfully. As we've seen in previous chapters, genuine giving cannot include the internal attitude of sorrow, regret, or reluctance ("grudgingly"). Neither can it occur under external pressure or coercion ("compulsion") that binds you to a legalistic, arbitrary amount. God does not love that kind of giver, but He does love the one whose heart is thrilled and overjoyed at the prospect of investing in His kingdom.

Generosity from God

The second harvest benefit for the Christian who sows bountifully is *generosity from God*. "And God is able to make all grace abound to you, so that always having all sufficiency in everything, you may have an abundance for every good deed" (2 Cor. 9:8).

The apostle Paul writes "God is able," because He has all the power in the universe to be generous to those who are generous to Him. It is precisely that power which is the ground of our confidence that He will fulfill His promise to be generous. God's ability is the starting point that helps us believe that giving away all we have is worth the apparent risk. After all, in the natural realm, giving away something results in having less. So, believing that you will prosper in the spiritual realm by giving much away requires confidence and faith.

Giving God all your resources will not be foolhardy if you understand God's power and ability and realize that your faith must rest on Him, not on the wisdom of men

(1 Cor. 2:5). Redemptive history has thoroughly tested and proved God's ability to be abundantly generous and completely sufficient for believers' needs. For example, God completely vindicated Daniel's three friends' supreme faith in His power (Dan. 3:16–30). The Bible elsewhere describes the supernatural power they gave testimony to in verse 17 as incomparable (Exod. 15:11–12), incomprehensible (Job 26:14), great (Ps. 79:11), strong (Ps. 89:13), irresistible (Dan. 4:35), sovereign (Rom. 9:21), and without limits (Gen. 18:14; Matt. 19:26; Eph. 3:20).

We simply need to be more like Abraham, whose faith is described in Romans 4:21, "And being fully assured that what God had promised, He was able also to perform." God's promise to generously reward our giving is clearly contained in 2 Corinthians 9:8. Scripture in countless places demonstrates His ability to fulfill that promise or perform anything within the scope of His purpose.

Paul has such confidence in God's ability to be generous to those who give that he says God returns our generosity with abounding grace. Since God possesses infinite grace, He has every bit of it available to reimburse us in abundance. And exactly what is abounding grace in this context? It primarily refers to earthly wealth and provisions. Paul is expanding on the agricultural analogy of the harvest. If you sow material goods, you'll get material goods from God in return. If you give your money and possessions to God, He will lavish material goods back to you. The principle is simple: The generous giver will always have plenty. As someone once wrote, "As regularly as the resources of the cheerful giver are taxed by his generous giving, they are replenished by divine grace."

Paul further makes his point concerning God's abounding grace to us by borrowing a Greek philosophical term, the word that's translated "sufficiency" in 2 Corinthians 9:8. In ethical discussions, the Stoics used the word to refer to the proud independence of self-sufficiency that results in true happiness and contentment. But the apostle tells the Corinthians and us that the supposed self-sufficiency we often seek will be supplied by God, and we'll be content in having everything we need (cf. Phil. 4:19).

The reason God so sufficiently and overwhelmingly gives back to us is that His generosity might spur us on to do more good deeds. When God finds a generous giver, He sets a special love in that person and abundantly replenishes his or her resources so they can give even more. If we are faithful and consistent givers, God will establish a constant flow of blessing so that the more we give the more we'll have and the more we'll be able to engage in new opportunities to help others.

Paul's concluding instruction in 2 Corinthians 9:8 is solidly based on what God taught His people in the Old Testament,

> You shall generously give to him [your poor brother], and your heart shall not be grieved when you give to him, because for this thing the Lord your God will bless you in all your work and in all your undertakings. For the poor will never cease to be in the land; therefore I command you, saying, 'You shall freely open your hand to your brother, to your needy and poor in your land'" (Deut. 15:10–11).

So the Lord long ago promised to bless and prosper all the enterprises of the obedient, generous givers—not so they will become rich and consume that prosperity on their own desires, but so they can continue to give and thereby perform good deeds in meeting others' needs.

To further underscore that his teachings on giving are not

novel ideas, Paul refers directly and indirectly to other Old Testament verses. Second Corinthians 9:9 is a direct quote of Psalm 112:9, "As it is written, 'He scattered abroad, he gave to the poor, his righteousness endures forever.'" The godly man gave generously to the poor and God remembered his righteous deeds, replenishing him and rewarding him both in time and eternity (cf. Hos. 10:12).

In verse 10, Paul paraphrases a portion of Isaiah 55:10 as he reiterates the principle of the harvest benefit, "Now He who supplies seed to the sower and bread for food will supply and multiply your seed for sowing and increase the harvest of your righteousness." The same God who faithfully provides everything His creatures need and is kind to all men—especially to believers—will in an extra gracious way reward His children who give generously. The Lord never fails in His unwavering, reliable provision and promise to us.

An eternal reward of righteousness is the ultimate expression of God's generosity to the one who gives all. But temporal blessings also reflect His generosity. Such generosity is in the here and now because the Lord loves a cheerful giver and specially blesses him (Prov. 3:9–10; 10:22; 28:27).

Glory to God

In 2 Corinthians 9:11–13, the apostle Paul brings us to the heart of the issue concerning God's harvest benefits:

> You will be enriched in everything for all liberality, which through us is producing thanksgiving to God. For the ministry of this service is not only fully supplying the needs of the saints, but is also overflowing through many thanksgivings to God. Because of the proof given by this ministry, they will glorify God for your obedience to your confession of the

gospel of Christ and for the liberality of your contribution to
them and to all.

When Paul, Titus, and their companions took the special
offering to the Jerusalem church, the believers there would
thank and worship God for meeting their needs through the
gifts of other saints. Any time one group of believers shows
real generosity to another group of believers, the recipients
will thank God for prompting the hearts of the givers. So the
third great benefit of sowing bountifully is that *your giving
will touch more people and they will give all the more glory and
thanks to God.*

Paul viewed the whole process of the special collection as
a spiritual, priestly service ("the ministry of this service") that
was definitely going to meet the needs of the recipients
("fully supplying" in the Greek is a double intensive for
emphasis).

In addition to meeting basic physical needs, the collection
resulted in two spiritual benefits. First, it overflowed in many
thanksgivings to God, which is really central to the idea of giving glory to God through our giving. Second, it proved to the
Jerusalem church that the Corinthians were genuinely saved
("the proof given by this ministry"). Second Corinthians 9
assumes that some of the Jewish believers doubted the reality
of the Gentiles' salvation, particularly in view of the sin and
chaos that had occurred at Corinth. But if the Jews were looking for some evidence to verify the Corinthians' salvation,
they had to look no further than "the liberality of your contribution to them." Likewise, when you or I give magnanimously
and lovingly from the heart, it gives evidence of our regeneration while it touches the lives of others and glorifies God.

Friends from God

The fourth, and perhaps most tangible, harvest benefit to any generous Christian is *friends from God*, "while they also, by prayer on your behalf, yearn for you because of the surpassing grace of God in you" (2 Cor. 9:14, NASB). By praying for the Corinthians, which was all they could really afford to give back, the poor Jewish believers revealed their friendship for those who would give to meet their needs. Those who receive your gifts recognize that God is at work in your life, long for fellowship with you, and pray for you. In short, when you give in obedience to God's plan, one of the benefits He returns to you is the blessing of new friends.

We should all desire that friends, old and new, would be praying for us. The prayers of friends on our behalf knit our hearts to theirs—mutual prayer is the stuff of real unity in the church. (True unity is first built around sound doctrine, but it's practically manifested in those brethren you pray for, and those who pray for you.) When we reach out with our giving and meet others' needs, something profound and precious occurs—they become friends who pray for us, because that's how love works in the body of Christ.

Jesus began His conclusion to the parable of the unjust steward with these fascinating, but somewhat enigmatic, statements: "And his master praised the unrighteous manager because he had acted shrewdly; for the sons of this age are more shrewd in relation to their own kind than the sons of light. And I say to you, make friends for yourselves by means of the wealth of unrighteousness, so that when it fails, they will receive you into the eternal dwellings" (Luke 16:8–9, NASB). The manager (steward) was using money to make friends of his master's debtors by discounting their debts. He wanted them to be obligated to him so that he might be able to stay in their homes, if need be, after being fired by the master.

Jesus, while not condoning the manager's dishonesty to his master, indicated that the unjust manager was smarter than most believers, because he knew how to get the long-term benefit from this world's wealth. We should learn from the manager's example and invest the Lord's money in ways that advance His kingdom, bring sinners to salvation, and assist fellow believers in need. Such generosity leads us to make new friends on earth whom we will forever fellowship with later in heaven—and all will be part of the benefits of God's gracious harvest to those of us who give away our resources with eternity in view.

Likeness to God

The apostle Paul's most climactic, uplifting statement in his instruction about the benefits of God's harvest is in 2 Corinthians 9:15, "Thanks be to God for His indescribable gift!" It's obvious that the "indescribable gift" is Jesus Christ. He is the gift that inspires all other gifts (cf. Rom. 8:32), the gift so immense and glorious that human language can't describe it. But how does Paul's short benediction relate to the benefits of giving? The answer is quite simple.

God's example in giving us His only begotten Son laid the foundation for all Christian giving. When we give gener-ously, we are like God. Paul's final crescendo of praise suggests the final benefit of giving, the final aspect of the true path to prosperity—*we exhibit our likeness to God.*

In looking ahead to His death, Jesus told the disciples, "Truly, truly, I say to you, unless a grain of wheat falls into the earth and dies, it remains alone; but if it dies, it bears much fruit" (John 12:24). God planted the grain, embodied in the gift of His Son, in the grave ("the earth") and reaped much fruit, a redeemed people for Himself. If it were not for that great truth, accomplished solely by God's sovereign grace, we would not even be able to sow and reap through our giving. And we are most like Him when we give voluntarily, sacrificially, and joyfully that others may benefit.

In another epistle, Paul exhorts us to be imitators of God in everything (Eph. 5:1)—which certainly includes giving, and he also cites Christ's sacrificial death as the ultimate example to us of self-sacrifice (v. 2). In view of that, how can you and I possibly consider it too difficult to sow our resources as broadly and generously as possible? After all, such giving simply results in our being more and more like God, and less and less like the world.

It is my prayer that the various topics and issues we've explored in this book—all through the lens of Scripture—will have a permanent impact on your life. I trust that the principles we've highlighted and the conclusions we've drawn will bring your attitude toward money and your practices of giving ever closer to God's standard.

As a concluding illustration, consider 1 Kings 17:8–16 and this unforgettable story of God's provision during the ministry of Elijah:

> Then the word of the LORD came to him, saying, "Arise, go to Zarephath, which belongs to Sidon, and stay there; behold, I have commanded a widow there to provide for you." So he arose and went to Zarephath, and when he came to the gate of the city, behold, a widow was there gathering sticks; and he called to her and said, "Please get me a little water in a jar, that I may drink." As she was going to get it, he called to her and said, "Please bring me a piece of bread in your hand." But she said, "As the LORD your God lives, I

have no bread, only a handful of flour in the bowl and a little oil in the jar; and behold, I am gathering a few sticks that I may go in and prepare for me and my son, that we may eat it and die." Then Elijah said to her, "Do not fear; go do as you have said, but make me a little bread cake from it first and bring it out to me, and afterward you may make one for yourself and for your son. For thus says the LORD God of Israel, 'The bowl of flour shall not be exhausted, nor shall the jar of oil be empty, until the day that the LORD sends rain on the face of the earth.'" So she went and did according to the word of Elijah, and she and he and her household ate for many days. The bowl of flour was not exhausted nor did the jar of oil become empty, according to the word of the LORD which He spoke through Elijah.

If God promises in His Word to fill your jar, he'll fill your jar (cf. Isa. 48:17). The question for you then becomes, When God says if you give He'll fill your jar to overflowing with the benefits of His harvest, do you really believe that? If you are generous according to the biblical model and characteristics of giving, you will never lack what you need. But you have to exercise faith and manage your resources with integrity. Then when you give lavishly, you'll reap a rich bounty from God Himself.

 *Appendix*

The Seductive Fantasy of Gambling

THE SUBJECT OF GAMBLING is so often overlooked, not discussed, or at the very least, insufficiently addressed within the church. But in view of the huge popularity and widespread prominence of state lotteries and other increasingly popular forms of gambling—and the pressure in today's culture to utilize all available moneymaking methods and get-rich-quick formulas—I believe it's vital in a book on money, stewardship, and giving to include a brief discussion of gambling.

WHAT IS GAMBLING?

Sometimes the best way to get a grasp on a topic, especially if it's the least bit controversial, is to understand what it is not. Gambling is not merely taking a risk on something. That would be an overly simplistic definition because *everything* in life involves risk. Life itself is uncertain, as the apostle James reminds us, "You do not know what your life will be like tomorrow. You are just a vapor that appears for a little while and then vanishes away. Instead, you ought to say, 'If the

Lord wills, we will live and also do this or that'" (James 4:14–15). There are many legitimate labors, activities, and investments that have risk attached to them, but they are not gambling. That's because the risk is associated with reasonable, wise, and manageable processes and rewards.

For example, there is risk in farming. The farmer basically invests all his money in the soil with the hope that he'll harvest fivefold or more on his investment when the crops have grown. But if the climate turned unfavorable during the growing season, or global market factors reduced crop prices, the farmer could suffer big financial losses.

Likewise, there is financial risk in any number of endeavors. A new company might fail because the market research for your product was overly optimistic. Spending money for further education might prove fruitless because the market for your specialty may have evaporated when you graduate. Investing in the stock market can be uncertain because some previously strong stock options may experience drastic reversals. Owning property can be unpredictable—the real estate market may cause your house to rise in value, or drop sharply. Owning insurance also involves risks (you're hedging against the unknown, and usually you won't need to file a claim very often).

In all those areas, the risk involves rational choices based on a track record to which you can apply your wisdom and experience and retain a measure of control. But that's not true with gambling.

The terms *gamble, gambling, gambler* originate from the Old English word *gammon,* which denoted the basic concept of a game. Gambling is a game that goes beyond normal risk, skill, reason, and controllable factors. It is based on sheer chance, randomness without skill, or one's personal involvement. It's not like normal competition, in which you strive for a prize by producing something better, by accomplishing something sooner, or by doing something more efficiently. Those are rational, manageable, controllable activities.

In contrast, gambling is an activity in which a person, in the hope of winning something of greater value, risks something of value to forces of chance completely beyond his or her control or rational expectation. And incredibly, gambling is often accompanied by the notion that the longer you engage in it, the better your odds become of succeeding. But sheer random chance never changes its odds, because there are no elements you can control to increase your likelihood of winning.

GAMBLING'S RECENT TRENDS AND EFFECTS

America is on a gambling binge. (That is also true in many other Western nations, and many of the following facts and conclusions apply in those societies as well.) It is the invisible addiction assaulting millions of people in the United States and around the world. It's hard to calculate exactly how much money is wagered each year in the United States on gambling, but a reasonable estimate would place the total at *one trillion dollars*—five hundred billion on legal gambling and another five hundred billion on illegal gambling. The best statistics indicate that about ten million Americans are compulsive gamblers, and that's more than the total number of alcoholics. Gambling is gaining rapidly in popularity and acceptability, and it is appearing in so many convenient formats (lottery machines at every convenience store and gas station, video slot machines, card clubs, off-track wagering on horse and dog racing, the Internet, and betting on athletic events) that its total financial impact on society is becoming difficult to calculate.

Between 1894 and 1964, there was no government-sponsored gambling in America. Then in 1964, New Hampshire became the first state in more than a century to sponsor a lottery. Now more than two-thirds of the states plus the District of Columbia sponsor lotteries. There are also more than five hundred casinos across the country, many operated by Native Americans with the benefit of generous government tax breaks.

According to surveys, by 1974, 61 percent of Americans were wagering more than 47 billion dollars annually. Fifteen years later those figures were up to 71 percent and 246 billion dollars, respectively. By 1995, the figures had soared to 95 percent participation, at an annual outlay of 500 billion dollars. Recent figures say that on the Nevada slot machines alone people spend 5 billion dollars every year. Ninety-two million American households visit casinos each year, and 10 percent of total American wages is thrown away annually in gambling. I find these statistics utterly mind-boggling but, sad to say, not all that surprising.

That's because during the past thirty years the rise of legalized gambling has followed the general trend in American culture toward permissiveness, pornography, drug and alcohol abuse, and materialism. Casino gambling is no longer confined to its west coast and east coast enclaves of Las Vegas, Nevada, and Atlantic City, New Jersey. With Native American and riverboat casinos, it is accessible right outside conservative, small-town communities in Middle America. Now people can also gamble at home via the Internet, with a rapidly increasing number of gambling sites. Annual gambling expenditures now exceed the amount spent on films, books, and entertainment combined; and it exceeds the combined total spent for tickets to major sporting events.

The societal effect of this huge surge in gambling has been extremely negative. First of all, it has exploited the poor, uneducated, and undisciplined sectors of the population. The gambling enterprise provides wealth for a comparative handful of people at the expense of the less-affluent masses. People in the lowest income bracket spend four times as much of their salaries on gambling as do those in higher income brackets.

In my view it is unthinkable that governments, which are supposed to protect citizens and maintain public order, should allow the exploitation of the working poor by state-supported gambling. On the one hand, governments say they must give welfare benefits and tax breaks to the poor by taxing the wealthier people. And on the other hand governments hypocritically fund and promote gambling (most notably, state lotteries) that takes money right out of the hands of those who can least afford to lose it. This all happens under the cynical and seductive guise that thousands of people will get rich. Instead, gambling's net effects on the poor are: increased debt, devalued work, harm to marital and family unity, and damage to emotional and physical health.

The standard propaganda in support of legalized gambling in a community has always been that it promotes business and economic development. But the harsh reality is that it doesn't do that at all. Instead of alleviating social and economic ills, gambling generates more of them. For example, since Atlantic City legalized casino gambling in 1976, its population has declined 20 percent. The crime rate has increased 380 percent and consequently the police force has doubled. Unemployment has increased significantly, and 50 percent of the city's two thousand, one hundred businesses have closed. Four of the past six mayors have been indicted for corruption; three are currently serving jail terms. One writer aptly summarized the situation, "Atlantic City used to be the slum by the sea. Now it's a slum by the sea with casinos."

As Atlantic City's experience suggests, gambling promotes

crime of all sorts, especially organized crime. In a 1989 report, the New Jersey Casino Control Commission reported huge increases in the numbers of assaults, rapes, prostitution activity, and drug deals. All of those activities are either controlled by organized crime or are the direct results of increased street crime. No matter what type of criminal, the presence of casino gambling in a city attracts large numbers of new offenders to the community.

Nevada, for a long time the only state in America with legalized casinos, reports the highest incarceration rate in the nation. Forty percent of those in jail are from out of state, which again indicates the attractiveness of gambling to criminals. Nevada also has the dubious distinctions of the highest bankruptcy rate and the largest per capita consumption of alcohol of any state in the United States. (Casinos provide free liquor to customers because studies have shown that intoxicated people gamble more.) In 1994 the FBI found that Las Vegas had the worst ratio of violent crimes committed to violent crimes solved of any large city in the country—five to one!

THE CHURCH'S POSITION ON GAMBLING

In the wake of the many ill effects gambling has wrought upon modern society, one might reasonably ask, "Where has the church been in all of this?" Unfortunately, any informed believer would have to reply, "It's been absent." Concerning social issues, the evangelical church in recent decades has been more involved in antiabortion, antipornography, pro-family values, and proconservative electoral issues. (Those activities are legitimate, as long as they don't replace preaching the gospel as the church's number one priority.) But the church has spoken out very little and done virtually nothing in opposition to the pervasive presence and influence of gambling. Government, especially on the state level, is an advocate for gambling, and the church needs to take a stand, expose the evils of gambling, and declare how it's really at odds with the principles of Scripture.

Because the Bible contains no proof-texts that explicitly say, "Thou shalt not gamble," Christians have perhaps backed off, thinking it was too difficult to make a case against gambling. Furthermore, I think the church has not spoken out on the bad effects of gambling because individual gamblers don't exhibit obvious physical evidences of those symptoms. You can usually see the outward ill effects when an individual is high on alcohol or drugs. But that's not true of people deeply involved in gambling. Gamblers can appear as respectable and normal as anyone else. Finally, there has been ignorance of the gambling industry's nature and background and an ignorance of the biblical principles that indicate what's wrong with gambling.

Any believer who aspires to be a wise steward of his or her resources and a faithful advocate of the truth needs to address the disturbing sin of gambling. The ancient church certainly did. An unknown preacher in second-century North Africa, probably in or near Alexandria, delivered the following sermon, which gives us some good insight into how the early church viewed gambling.

Christians: great and abundant is the Lord's mercy. Satan's temptations are numerous, but the principle ones among them are idolatry, fornication, theft, extortion, greed, fraud, drunkenness, impatience, adultery, murder, jealousy, false witness, lying, envying, wrath, slander, heresy and a thousand other crimes like them. And of this number is gambling.

The game of dice is an obvious snare of the devil. He presides over the game in person, bringing to it the deadly venom of the serpent and even inducing ruin which, when it is seen to be nothing, a great letdown is brought about in the players. I ask you, O Christians, why is the former the case? This hand has been purified from its sins which were committed prior to conversion and the same hand has been admitted to the Lord's table, having received by God's mercy that which concerns the salvation of the soul. The same hand that rolls the dice is lifted up to the Lord in prayer. What shall we say when the very hand with which we make the sign of the cross on our forehead and with which we consume the Lord's table is involved again in the devil's noose from which it formerly had been delivered? I speak of this hand which is always given over to gambling, causing its ruin and damnation. This hand is accustomed to the unbridled passion of gambling because gambling is like the devil's hunting sphere and those who play the dice are wounded with an irresistible allurement.

It is at the gambling table, I tell you, it is at the gambling table where the devil slyly watches for the moment when he shall surprise the players and immediately rejoice in his triumph over his victim. I tell you, it is at the gambling table where one loses his possessions and enormous sums of money. The loss leads him into court battles and insane passions of theft. O noxious gamblers, you are pernicious and filled with indolent iniquity. O cruel hands which turn their own arms against themselves, ruining with disgraceful zeal the estate which their ancestors have amassed by the sweat of their brow. O savaged hands that run to the dice, guilty and indefatigable, applying themselves day and night without leave. You damn yourselves by your sin, yet after you have committed it you do not stop.

The gambling board is the devil's snare and the enemy's

trap which entices greed but in actuality brings utter ruin. By gambling, men become poor, squandering their own riches. Stop being a dice player and start being a Christian before Christ, beneath the gaze of the angels and in the presence of the martyrs. Cast your money upon the altar of the Lord, distribute your money to the poor before you allow it to be squandered by your unruly passions and trust your stakes to Christ who is always victorious. Divert all your fortune and surplus for the necessities of the church. Deposit your gold and silver and your riches in heavenly treasure. Snatch your hands back from the sacrifices of the devil. Break away from these unruly customs and pursue being a self-controlled Christian. Apply yourself to wisdom and teach yourself in the counsels of the gospel. Lift pure hands to Christ, no longer look upon the dice. Amen.

That hard-hitting message shows how opposed some leaders in the early church were to the vice of gambling. Centuries later the key leaders of the Reformation also took clear stands against gambling. John Calvin outlawed gambling in the entire city of Geneva, Switzerland, and Martin Luther declared, "Money won by gambling is not won without self-seeking and sin." I see no reason that we should not be fully persuaded to stand against gambling, just as our ancestors in the faith did.

WHY GAMBLING IS WRONG

To understand the immorality and sinfulness of gambling completely, it's crucial that we understand some relevant biblical principles. But first we need to be clear on something that's contained in Scripture but often misunderstood and misapplied concerning the issue of gambling.

Not Justified by the Casting of Lots

Some believers want to justify gambling as a modern counterpart to the casting of lots. They reason that because people cast lots during biblical times the Bible must affirm the role of gambling. But is that an accurate understanding of what lots were?

It is true that lots functioned much like dice. They were made of sheep's knuckle bones of various shapes and sizes, and the roll of those bones indicated a certain meaning. Ancient lots were used in some nongambling games as well as in games of chance, however, people have made the long-term association between lots and gambling. Therefore, some believers have equated gambling with lots and assumed that because God sometimes used lots, gambling is not necessarily wrong.

A brief survey of references to lots in Scripture will clarify their true nature and purpose in Bible times. The casting of lots was used to make decisions (cf. Exod. 28:30; Lev. 8:8; Num. 27:21; 1 Sam. 28:6), to select animals for sacrifice (Lev. 16:7–10), to choose soldiers for battle (Judg. 20:18), to identify the holder of forbidden loot (Josh. 7:14–18), to determine that Jonathan had violated the king's oath (1 Sam. 14:41–43), to identify Jonah as the cause of a storm (Jonah 1:7), and to choose Matthias to replace Judas as an apostle (Acts 1:26).

Those and other examples simply affirm that lots were used to determine certain matters. But at no time in the casting of lots did anyone ever put something of value at risk. Therefore those instances of casting lots were not examples of gambling. Proverbs 16:33 puts the issue into perspective very well, "The lot is cast into the lap, but its every decision is from the Lord." Lots were simply a way by which a sovereign God providentially revealed His will. When the people had to make an important decision and had difficulty ascertaining God's will, He sovereignly intervened and caused the lots to fall in such a way as to tell His followers what to do. There was no fate, chance, or luck involved.

After Acts 1:26, Scripture records no further use of lots to discover God's will. We now have the indwelling Holy Spirit and God's written Word to guide us in knowing His perfect will. The practice of casting lots is no longer necessary.

Clearly, the casting of lots, as described in Scripture, was not gambling and therefore cannot at all be a rationale for any contemporary practice of gambling. The ancient use of lots is more closely parallel to the modern practice of drawing straws. Even though the term *lottery* comes from *lot*, contemporary lotteries are qualitatively different from the simple casting of lots. Lotteries work on the basis of random chance, whereas lots succeeded by God's sovereign purpose working through the providential toss of the lots.

Denies the Reality of God's Sovereignty

Perhaps the primary reason gambling is wrong is that, by affirming the existence of luck or chance, it denies the reality of a sovereign God. The Bible, however, clearly and repeatedly teaches that God is the sovereign of the universe (e.g., Gen. 1:1; Deut. 29:29; Job 37:9–13; Ps. 33:11; 39:5; 104:5–9; Isa. 40:13–14; 50:2; Dan. 4:35; Rom. 8:28–29; Eph. 1:9–11; Col. 1:16–17). In that role, He miraculously (by suspending natural law) and providentially (by operating through natural law) controls every detail of every event to accomplish His own purposes.

Chance, the major premise of gambling's outworking, is the fabric of a human imagination that wants to deny the existence of a sovereign God. But Psalm 103:19 says, "The

Lord has established His throne in the heavens, and His sovereignty rules over all." To practice the idolatry of gambling is detestable to God, because whatever happens to us and whatever we receive is according to His sovereign purpose and plan. To rely on the nonexistent god of chance or luck to alter those realities is just sinful folly.

Built on Irresponsible Stewardship

Gambling is also wrong because it is not sound, responsible stewardship of what God has given us. The psalmist writes, "The earth is the LORD's, and all it contains, the world, and those who dwell in it" (Ps. 24:1; cf. 50:10–12). Nothing we have really belongs to us; it belongs to God, and we should use all of it to His glory (cf. Matt. 6:19–21; 1 Cor. 10:31).

Jesus illustrates the command for good stewardship in His parable of the talents in Matthew 25:14–30. In the story, the owner of an estate tested the stewardship of three servants during a time he was away from them. Before he went on a journey, the owner distributed five talents (a measure of silver) to one, two to another, and one to a third servant, all in an effort to see how the servants would manage what they received.

The first two servants faithfully invested their talents and doubled their monies. But the third servant took his one talent and merely buried it in the ground. When the master returned from his journey, he rewarded the faithful servants. But he rebuked and punished the servant who was not a good steward:

> You wicked, lazy slave . . . you ought to have put my money
> in the bank, and on my arrival I would have received my
> money back with interest. Therefore take away the talent

from him, and give it to the one who has the ten talents. For to everyone who has, more shall be given, and he will have an abundance; but from the one who does not have, even what he does have shall be taken away. Throw out the worthless slave into the outer darkness; in that place there will be weeping and gnashing of teeth. (vv. 26–30)

The lazy, timid servant should have made something of the money entrusted to him (cf. 1 Cor. 4:2). God is not content that we just keep what we have. He wants us to use it for His honor and glory. If that servant was sent to hell simply because he kept his money and didn't invest it, what's going to happen to people like habitual gamblers who waste what they have? The worst possible stewardship of God's resources is for someone to throw them away at the altar of a god called chance or luck. It's idolatry of the worst sort.

Erodes the Biblical Work Ethic

God didn't assign work to mankind simply because it was good for Him. He gave it to us because it was a blessing to a fallen people who needed to be preoccupied with something better than constant temptation to sin. We are to earn our bread by the sweat of our brows (Gen. 3:19; cf. Exod. 20:9). Proverbs 12:11 clearly sets forth the contrast between a godly and an ungodly work ethic: "He who works his land will have abundant food, but he who chases fantasies lacks judgment"(NIV). Gambling is a prime example of someone chasing fantasies. Like fools, people throw their money away to random chance, with astronomically slim possibilities of some day actually winning more money in return. At the same time, the addictive wagering process causes them to disdain honest hard work.

Irresponsibility in the realm of work is an abdication of one of the basic definitions of personhood. And for the Christian, it means abandonment and disobedience toward a basic God-given duty (Eph. 4:28; Col. 3:23; 2 Thess. 3:10–12; 1 Tim. 5:8). God's world is a place of order and purpose, not a place of chaos that operates according to the whims of chance. He wants us to use our reasoning ability, perform work that honors Him, and enjoy the blessings that result.

Driven by the Sin of Covetousness

Gambling violates the tenth commandment, which says, "You shall not covet your neighbor's house; you shall not covet your neighbor's wife or his male servant or his female servant or his ox or his donkey or anything that belongs to your neighbor" (Exod. 20:17). Gambling and its accompanying greediness encourage the sin of covetousness. But Jesus warned, ". . . Beware, and be on your guard against every form of greed; for not even when one has an abundance does his life consist of his possessions" (Luke 12:15). Greed and covetousness soon lead to the sin of discontent, which directly violates the apostle Paul's statement in Philippians 4:11–12, "I have learned to be content in whatever circumstances I am. I know how to get along with humble means, and I also know how to live in prosperity."

Gambling's persistent appeal to covetousness is fundamentally opposed to the unselfishness taught in Scripture. It continually assumes that God has not given us what we ought to have and that there is somehow more wealth that will finally make us happy. But Proverbs 30:7–8 reveals the fallacy of such thinking, "Two things I asked of You, do not refuse me before I die: keep deception and lies far from me, give me neither poverty nor riches; feed me with the food that is my portion." God knows you and me and what's best for us and what tests we need to shape our characters. The idol of gambling only detracts from that picture and leads people down the path of unbelief and disobedience (v. 9).

Built on the Exploitation of Others

Finally, gambling is wrong because it exploits people who can least afford to be victims. Actually in a not-so-subtle fashion it violates the eighth commandment, "You shall not steal" (Exod. 20:15). For everyone who wins something at gambling, there are millions of losers—people who have been duped by the seductive marketing appeal of gambling and prompted to throw away large sums of money. So often such victims are the less educated working class, the elderly, or undisciplined young people.

Gambling not only drains the basic economic provision from people (wives and children don't have necessities), but also undermines philanthropic giving. Instead of using discretionary money to help the poor and needy, those who gamble waste their discretionary money in selfish, largely futile attempts to strike it rich. Essentially such behavior fosters the sin of not loving your neighbor as yourself. If people are heavily into gambling, they will not give generously to others, nor will they be there to help relieve the financial distress of a needy neighbor. In short, gambling exploits and victimizes the most vulnerable.

I believe there is no escaping the fact that gambling is wrong, unscriptural, anti-God, and seductive to millions of people in our society. It lures them into habits of squandering their money on the false hope that their odds are only going to get better and "pay day" is just around the corner.

Legalized gambling derives from postmodern pessimism, hopelessness, and moral relativism. It says that success in life results from random chance and "luck," and the ability to place a smart wager.

Even though some form of gambling is legal just about everywhere, it has no place in the life of a believer. If you are not involved in this sin, continue to refrain from it. If you are engaged in some form of gambling, repent of it and receive God's forgiveness. When it comes to the legitimacy of gambling, you ought to operate in the spirit of 1 Corinthians 6:12, "All things are lawful for me, but not all things are profitable. All things are lawful for me, but I will not be mastered by anything."

Study Guide

CHAPTER 1
THE MORALITY OF MONEY

Summarizing the Chapter

Because whatever wealth we have comes from a sovereign God, we can trust Him to meet our basic needs and give us victory over materialism.

Getting Started (Choose One)

1. Why do you think materialism is such a temptation for people in contemporary Western culture? Discuss two or three primary causes. Is the average person concerned about these?
2. How do you struggle most in your attitude toward money? Why do you think that's true?

Answering the Questions

1. What percentage of Jesus' parables teaches something about handling our resources?
2. What are three topics to which the Bible makes fewer references than it does to wealth?

3. Morally speaking, what is the nature of money?

4. How do some well-meaning Christians view money? What is sometimes their remedy for that "problem?" Does Scripture support that solution?

5. Under what conditions has God granted us stewardship of money and possessions (see Deut. 8:18; Hag. 2:8)?

6. What sinful attitude toward money has captured the thinking of many in the church during the past several generations?

7. What practical thoughts and actions can help you overcome the temptation of materialism?

8. What three scriptural truths regarding wealth and possessions can help us attain true contentment?

Focusing on Prayer

• Spend some time in prayer today thanking God for whatever wealth and possessions He has graciously given to you.

• Is there some part of your resources that you have not relinquished to God's control? If so, repent of that attitude and give Him complete control of everything you have.

Applying the Truth

Memorize Deuteronomy 8:18.

CHAPTER 2:
GUIDELINES AND WARNINGS ABOUT MONEY

Summarizing the Chapter

If you heed the Bible's clear guidelines about money and avoid the sinful symptoms of loving money, you will demonstrate genuine salvation and a healthy relationship with God.

Getting Started (Choose One)

1. Have you ever resented being subject to a dress code at school or work? Did you ever feel restricted by guidelines on your behavior? Were some of those rules actually beneficial in the long run? How?
2. Has greed for making money affected the way people perform their jobs these days? Recall an instance when that attitude detracted from the quality of professional service you received.

Answering the Questions

1. What motivation in the workplace should supersede that of salary?
2. What truth is inherent in Jesus' admonitions about money and possessions in Matthew 6:33 and Luke 16:13?
3. What was the first area of Zaccheus' life that was transformed by the miracle of his conversion? Why was that so amazing in his case?
4. What prevented the rich man in Mark 10 from receiving eternal life?
5. What attitude toward wealth did the rich man in Luke 12:15–21 reveal? In what specific ways did he demonstrate it?

6. What does Mark 12:41 indicate about the way Jesus observes what we do in our giving?

7. What is the real issue Paul is warning about in 1 Timothy 6:10? How have people erroneously interpreted that verse?

8. What are five different signs that help us recognize a person who is a lover of money?

9. Write down four of the six negative effects of loving money. Include at least one Scripture reference with each.

10. Ultimately, what kind of behavior does extreme love of money lead to?

11. What was so exemplary about C. T. Studd's behavior concerning his personal wealth?

Focusing on Prayer

- Pray that the Lord would make you so faithful in your finances that no one could doubt your spiritual health and salvation.

- Do you know someone whose life seems controlled by the love of money? If so, pray for that individual and ask God for an opportunity to share with him or her what the Word says about materialism.

Applying the Truth

Examine your checkbook and other financial records for the past six months. Are there evidences that your spending patterns and priorities reflect a love of money and possessions? Perhaps you have spent too much on frivolous or inappropriate items and activities. Maybe you haven't invested enough in other areas (church giving, certain worthwhile ministries). Prayerfully resolve to adopt a new budget that better reflects

God's priorities, even if it means changing your habit in just one category of spending.

CHAPTER 3:
THE ESSENTIALS OF BIBLICAL STEWARDSHIP

Summarizing the Chapter

God has sovereignly given mankind stewardship over His creation. That means you can enjoy the world's natural resources and beauty, and exercise the privilege of acquiring money in God-honoring ways. Whatever amount of wealth God entrusts to you, He wants you to use it for His honor and glory.

Getting Started (Choose One)

1. How far should believers go in supporting environmental causes? Discuss the differences between prudent conservation of resources and contemporary "environmentalism."
2. What do you enjoy most about the kind of work you do? Why? How has reading this chapter changed your outlook toward work?

Answering the Questions

1. Briefly, what is the argument of those who advocate "Christian poverty"? How does an understanding of Jesus' real economic situation invalidate that view?
2. What distinction did God make between man and the rest of creation?
3. What will happen to the present world and how should that influence your enjoyment and use of its resources?

4. How has sin affected mankind's management of the earth's resources?

5. List at least four positive qualities of hard work.

6. What insect does the Book of Proverbs say is smarter than some humans?

7. What should be our overriding motivation in whatever type of work we do?

8. What is perhaps the most important aspect to keep in mind concerning savings?

9. Describe some ways modern advertising makes it difficult to maintain financial self-control. What is a good example of advertising's overemphasis on image?

10. What kinds of problems has the widespread use of credit cards created? What is the average balance the typical American household owes in credit card debt?

11. What is the wisdom of loaning money to others? Should we ever do it? What about the wisdom of countersigning for someone to borrow money? What does Scripture say?

Focusing on Prayer

- Thank the Lord for His generosity in providing a beautiful, resource-laden world for you to use and enjoy. Thank Him specifically for the ways He has allowed you to earn money and provide for yourself and others.

- Consider one of the areas of monetary stewardship that you might be weak in. Pray that God would help you be more disciplined and more scriptural in your handling of His resources.

Applying the Truth

Reread the many references from Proverbs contained in this chapter. Choose one for further study and meditation. Commit one of the passage's key verses to memory.

CHAPTER 4:
OUR TRUE RICHES ARE IN HEAVEN

Summarizing the Chapter

Christ in His Sermon on the Mount calls us to set our affections and invest our resources in eternal things, not to serve the master of temporal wealth and materialism.

Getting Started (Choose One)

1. Would you agree with the statement that all highly successful people are extremely single-minded? Discuss why or why not.
2. Have you ever worked two jobs at the same time (for example, day and evening)? How difficult was it to give proper focus and energy to both?

Answering the Questions

1. What erroneous doctrine did Jesus seek to correct in His teaching about heavenly treasures (Matt. 6:19–24)?
2. What is a person who hoards and stockpiles usually eager to do?
3. What are your strongest motives and desires inseparably connected to? What does that connection indicate about your faith in Christ?
4. How is the revival in Nehemiah 8–10 relevant to our attitudes about money?

5. What does the eye of Matthew 6:22 represent? Why is it so vital to keep it clear?
6. What other concept does the Greek term translated "masters" in Matthew 6:24 encompass besides the employer/employee relationship?

Focusing on Prayer

- Thank God that "heavenly security provides the only absolute safeguard for our treasures." Spend some extra time meditating on the ramifications of that truth.
- Pray that the Lord would give you a clear and single focus in all matters regarding money and possessions.

Applying the Truth

Read and study Nehemiah 8–9. Record your observations on how the people responded to Ezra's reading of God's Law. Make a list of all the good and bad memories the people recalled in chapter 9 as they confessed their sin. Is there some sin you need to confess, an attitude you need to forsake or adopt, or a practice you need to reinstitute concerning how you handle your wealth? Let Nehemiah 8–9 be a guide for you.

CHAPTER 5:
THE BIBLICAL MODEL FOR GIVING

Summarizing the Chapter

With Jesus' statements in Luke 6:38 and Acts 20:35 in mind, as well as the example of the Jerusalem church and Paul's model in 1 Corinthians 16:1–4, we should give generously, systematically, and sacrificially in our regular church offering and at every other opportunity.

Getting Started (Choose One)

1. When you were growing up, did you have a role model in the area of giving? If so, how has that helped you since? If not, what guidelines did you miss the most?

2. What do you anticipate most or appreciate best about the Sunday morning worship at your church? Why?

Answering the Questions

1. What did Jesus' symbolism in Luke 6:38 draw from?

2. What is the basic New Testament principle concerning giving and God's blessings?

3. What is unusual about Jesus' words in Acts 20:35?

4. What twofold issue confronts believers as a result of Christ's two promises on giving?

5. In what two basic areas of giving was the Jerusalem church a pacesetter?

6. Why were the pilgrim converts in the Jerusalem church so reluctant to leave after the Acts 2 Pentecost?

7. What was the main reason many of the pilgrims became impoverished? How easy was it for the Jewish believers to support them?

8. How did the persecution of Jewish believers at Jerusalem fulfill Jesus' words to the Twelve? Support your answer with Scripture.

9. What two economic factors further contributed to the Jerusalem church's poverty?

10. Acts 2:32–35 and 2:44–45 are often misinterpreted. Explain the true significance of what was going on in those passages.

11. Why did Paul make the Jerusalem church the object of a special offering project? Where in Scripture is the project first alluded to?
12. How systematic and regimented should the frequency of our church giving be? Is there room for flexibility?
13. What were the temple treasuries used for in New Testament times?
14. What should be the direct parallel between our giving and that of the Old Testament Israelites?

Focusing on Prayer

- Ask the Lord to help your church remain sound in its financial practices by following the pattern of the Jerusalem church.
- If you know of a church, a ministry, or an individual Christian worker (pastor, missionary) who is struggling financially, pray for them and consider giving a special gift to that need.

Applying the Truth

Reread Luke 6:38, Acts 20:35, and 1 Corinthians 16:2. Memorize one of them during the next week.

CHAPTER 6:
THE CHARACTERISTICS OF BIBLICAL GIVING

Summarizing the Chapter

The eight characteristics of biblical giving that the apostle Paul outlines in 2 Corinthians 8:1–8 are timeless guidelines for the ways genuine Christians will give.

Study Guide

Getting Started (Choose One)

1. Do you think prosperity makes people more willing to give or more inclined to be self-indulgent? Discuss.

2. When do you most appreciate having a set of guidelines for how to do something? Are they sometimes more of a hindrance than a help? When and why?

Answering the Questions

1. The churches in what first-century province exhibited excellent examples of biblical giving? In what three cities were they located?

2. What allows unregenerate people to do acts of human good? How do those good works compare to ones prompted by God's grace? Where can you often see examples of the contrast?

3. What difficult circumstances could have led the Macedonians to excuse themselves from any giving?

4. What was commentator R. C. H. Lenski's description of the Macedonians' giving attitude?

5. What two aspects of generosity did the Macedonians' giving exemplify?

6. What two characteristics does the phrase "beyond their ability" (2 Cor. 8:3) indicate about the amount of the Macedonians' giving?

7. Elaborate on how the original vocabulary of 2 Corinthians 8:4 proves the Macedonian's conviction that giving was a privilege.

8. What is the ultimate manifestation of giving by Christians (see Rom. 12:1-2)?

9. If biblical giving reveals true submission to God, what additional act of submission will it include?

10. If you're demonstrating all of the characteristics of biblical giving, what does that reveal about your Christian character and true motivation?

Focusing on Prayer

- Thank God for His matchless grace that allows you to invest in His kingdom.
- Does being faithful in giving sometimes become a burden to you? Ask the Lord's help in being more consistently joyful as you give.

Applying the Truth

Memorize Philippians 2:12–13 or 4:19. Write out the verse or verses in your own words and use them as incentives to improve one or more of the giving characteristics in which you are weak.

CHAPTER 7:
TITHING OR VOLUNTARY GIVING?

Summarizing the Chapter

Old Covenant *and* New Covenant patterns for giving include two varieties, required and voluntary. But in spite of many believers' understanding to the contrary, our giving should derive voluntarily from the heart, not from a fixed, mandatory percentage.

Getting Started (Choose One)

1. Have you ever changed your view on a nonessential but important issue, either biblical/doctrinal or secular? Briefly recall the process. What was the pivotal

piece of information that convinced you of the new viewpoint?

2. What's easier to comply with: a mandatory guideline, or an optional but strongly recommended guideline? Explain your answer.

Answering the Questions

1. What is the Old English derivation of the word *tithe*? What is the related meaning of the Greek and Hebrew equivalents?

2. Summarize in one or two sentences the typical argument in favor of tithing.

3. Briefly explain the three general reasons that the argument for tithing is seriously flawed.

4. Is the tithe a distinctly scriptural concept? How far back does the practice go, and what did it originally symbolize?

5. How early in Scripture were the first two recorded instances of mankind making offerings to God? Who made those offerings?

6. What motivated Abraham to make an offering to God in Genesis 12:7? What was the significance of his tithe in Genesis 14?

7. What modern phenomenon was the required giving in Genesis 41 and 47 a parallel to?

8. What was each of the three Mosaic tithes and what did each support? What was the total tithe and tax the Israelites were required to pay?

9. What characteristics of Old Testament voluntary giving matched those of New Testament times? What two giving occasions during the Law illustrate those principles?

10. What elements of the Jews' theocracy were still operative during Christ's time?

11. What did Jesus teach concerning payment of taxes? How did He illustrate it with Peter?

12. What do the only two uses of the word *tithe* in the Gospels refer to?

13. What obvious conclusion should we make concerning the Bible's teaching about tithing and the practice's applicability to us?

Focusing on Prayer

- Thank the Lord that the true basis of your giving to Him rests in the freedom of your heart's desire to do His will.

- Pray that others in your church or fellowship group would understand the true role of the tithe in Scripture and be free from any artificial bondage to giving a certain percentage.

Applying the Truth

Commit 2 Corinthians 9:6–7 to memory. Ask God for an opportunity to share the truth of these verses with someone who may be struggling with the issue of "tithing."

CHAPTER 8:
STEWARDSHIP WITH INTEGRITY

Summarizing the Chapter

Because many people are sensitive about giving and concerned that fundraising abuses not occur, the church must conduct any stewardship program with the highest integrity. The principles contained in 2 Corinthians 8:10—9:5 are excellent guides to ensure that your church does administer its stewardship with such integrity.

Getting Started (Choose One)

1. What is the first thing you look for to see if a store or company is reputable before doing business with it? Has there been a time recently when you should have been more careful before making a transaction? If so, describe what happened.

2. Do you think that welfare dependency would be decreased if church giving truly balanced the resources in the body of Christ? If so, why isn't such giving occurring to a greater degree?

Answering the Questions

1. What are two definitions of stewardship (dictionary and church-related)?

2. What two abusive episodes from recent history illustrate the need for voluntarism within any stewardship program?

3. What weakened the Corinthian believers' resolve to finish their initial commitment to Paul's special giving project?

4. According to Paul's critics, what was his real motivation in raising money for the Jerusalem church?

5. What is isostasy, and how does it relate to giving within the church?

6. What does Paul's reference to equality within the church *not* refer to? What common welfare abuse does it aim to avoid (see 2 Thess. 3:10)?

7. What are the real issues we should be concerned about regarding those persons leading any stewardship campaign?

8. What qualification do many churches today look for in a person who administrates the offering and other finances? Is that criterion necessarily or always wrong?

9. Why does it matter what unbelievers think regarding our conduct of a stewardship program?

10. What ultimate goal in giving should a church aim for as it seeks to be an example to others?

11. What other sins is covetousness synonymous with?

Focusing on Prayer

- Pray that the leaders in your church would always exhibit the highest biblical standards of integrity in overseeing its stewardship.

- Ask the Lord to guard your heart against covetousness so that such sin would never hinder your generous giving.

Applying the Truth

Go back over the list of questions to ask in evaluating a Christian fundraiser (at the end of the chapter). For each one, write a hypothetical example of what the question is seeking to guard against. For some, jot down additional comments that clarify the issues. Keep the list conveniently on file so you may refer to it the next time you encounter a solicitation from an unfamiliar organization that professes Christian values.

CHAPTER 9:
THE TRUE PATH TO PROSPERITY

Summarizing the Chapter

The biblical principle of sowing and reaping determines our prosperity: If we give as much as we can, we will reap the benefits of God's harvest and be considered wealthy in His eyes.

Getting Started (Choose One)

1. What is the worst or most foolish get-rich-quick scheme you ever heard about or were involved in? If you were actually involved, tell what you learned from the experience.
2. When society enjoys a period of economic prosperity, what do you think people appreciate most about it? What does the mere prospect of recession make you most concerned about? Why?

Answering the Questions

1. Give a one-sentence definition of the "prosperity gospel."
2. What does the generous Christian never need to fear?
3. What further meaning is inherent in the term "bountifully" in 2 Corinthians 9:6?
4. What group of believers does God reserve a special affection for?
5. What are at least four adjectives Scripture uses to describe God's supernatural power (include references)?
6. What does God desire that His generosity will motivate us to do?

7. To what does the apostle Paul refer in demonstrating that his teaching on God's generosity was not new with him?

8. Besides meeting the physical needs, what two spiritual benefits resulted from the special collection?

9. What is the twofold basis (philosophical and practical) for real church unity?

10. What lesson should we apply from the parable of the unjust steward to our giving practices?

11. What unfathomable example of divine giving laid the foundation for all subsequent giving by believers?

Focusing on Prayer

- Thank the Lord that His path to material and spiritual prosperity is so far superior to all other ways.

- Pray by name for those Christian friends you have made as a result of faithfulness in giving. Ask Him to continue to meet their needs and empower them for ministry.

Applying the Truth

Do a short study on God's promises of rewards to believers. Look up all the Scripture references we listed early in the chapter and identify for each the kind of reward promised. Compile a written list and use it as a reminder as you strive to be faithful to God's promised principle of sowing and reaping. Memorize one or two of the verses, as you are able.

Endnotes

Chapter One

1. John White, *The Golden Cow* (Downers Grove, Ill.: InterVarsity, 1979), 67–68; (italics in original).
2 Ibid., 89–90; (italics in original).

Chapter Two

1. Norman P. Grubb, *C. T. Studd: Cricketer and Pioneer* (London: Lutterworth Press, 1953), 65–66.

Chapter Three

1. Bill Bryson, "Secrets of the Fall," excerpted from his *I'm a Stranger Here Myself* (New York: Random House; Broadway Books), 1999, by *Reader's Digest,* October 1999, 97–98.
2. University of Michigan, Documents Center, *Statistical Resources on the Web,* "Federal/State Government Finances," online.

Chapter Four

1. Frederick Lewis Allen, *Only Yesterday* (New York: Bantam Books, 1959 reprint), 220, (emphasis in original).
2. G. Campbell Morgan, *The Gospel According to Matthew* (New York: Revell, 1929), 64–65.

Chapter Seven

1. Henry Brinton, "Do You Tithe? What We Owe Our Churches," *Los Angeles Times,* 19 October 1999, sec. E, p. 5.

Chapter Nine

1. For a more complete discussion, see my *Charismatic Chaos.* Grand Rapids: Zondervan, 1992, chap. 12.

Appendix

For much of the material in this appendix I am greatly indebted to Rex M. Rogers, *Seducing America: Is Gambling a Good Bet?* (Grand Rapids: Baker Book House, 1997), especially chapters 1–4.

Also available from
Dr. John F. MacArthur

How to Get the Most from God's Word

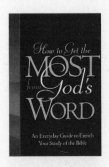

From one of today's most popular Bible speakers you can learn to effectively apply Bible teachings and principles to your own life. This practical Bible study companion cuts to the heart of God's Word and shows you how to do the same.

Introduction to Biblical Counseling

Solid theological foundations of biblical counseling are clearly presented in contrast to humanistic and secular theories of psychological counseling. A practical, proactive, and relevant book for students, church leaders, and lay people. This collection of writers represents some of America's leading biblical teachers and counselors.

The MacArthur Study Bible

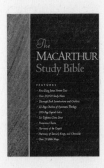

Featuring the word-for-word accuracy of the New King James Version, *The MacArthur Study Bible* is perfect for serious study. More than 20,000 study notes, a 200-page topical index and numerous charts, maps, outlines and articles create this classic work. Available in a variety of handsome bindings, including hardcover, indexed bonded leather, indexed genuine leather, and Moroccan leather. Winner of the "1998 Study Bible of the Year Award."

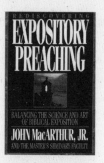

Rediscovering Expository Preaching

John MacArthur and his colleagues at The Master's Seminary offer a definitive manual on "rightly divining the Word of Truth" for today's congregations. With insight and clarity, they examine the four steps of Bible exposition, emphasizing the role of student and pastor in sermon preparation.

Rediscovering Pastoral Ministry

Encouraging, insightful, and challenging, *Rediscovering Pastoral Ministry* is designed for a new generation of shepherds who seek to lead with the passion of the apostles. Written by John MacArthur and his colleagues at The Master's Seminary, this guide outlines the biblical priorities essential to effective ministry.

What the Bible Says About Parenting

John MacArthur brings biblical parenting principles back to the table, showing parents how to rear their children with care, compassion, and common sense. He presents God-designed principles for transforming children's hearts toward a genuine desire for godliness and helps parents shepherd their children in making wise, godly choises by which to navigate life.

The Vanishing Conscience

In this compelling book, John MacArthur sounds a wake-up call for Christians to confront society's flight from moral responsibility and recognize sin for what it is. In doing so, he says, we can move from living a life of blame and denial to one of true peace and freedom.